Disciple Development Coaching

Christian Formation for the
21st Century

MARK TIDSWORTH
IRCEL HARRISON

© 2013

Published in the United States by Nurturing Faith Inc., Macon GA,
www.nurturingfaith.net.

Library of Congress Cataloging-in-Publication Data is available.

ISBN 978-1-938514-18-0

Contents

Foreword

If you are looking for a "program in a box/book" to transform your Christian education and discipleship programs at the congregational level, you will need to rethink your presuppositions as you read and work through the ideas in this pivotal work. A twentieth-century mentality will not carry you very far into the movement contemplated by Tidsworth and Harrison. This is an urgent call for the church to realign with the nature of the twenty-first-century world of which we are a part. If for no other reason, this book is a significant read.

The authors support their discussion with clear biblical and spiritual insights. The chapters also provide some good contemporary background from others who are writing and thinking about church development. Reading this book will help bring the reader up to date on leadership, church culture, change, and the general state of God's church in the twenty-first century.

All around us we hear moaning about how the church has lost its place in the world. *Disciple Development Coaching* is a highly relational movement that has the potential to empower all Christians to find their places in the world. It also locates the responsibility for the church's mission in the hands, hearts, and minds of all disciples.

The chapters are set forth in a highly linear and logical manner as the authors explain thoroughly their proposal. It is a "working read." The reader must place herself in the text and move through exercises in the context of a training manual. Yet, this is not a method or program. The entire foundation is relational, almost natural. One wonders why we didn't figure this out a long time ago.

The relationship between the coach and the disciple is a movement through conversation with a major emphasis on listening and empowering the disciple to develop competencies already available in his frame of Christian reference. The coach and the disciple ask, listen, explore, design, commit, and support in a shared experience that has a natural move back and forth. There is no beginning or end; it is a relational process that is part of an intentional long-term way of life.

As the authors state in the opening chapter: "Disciple Development Coaching is a way of thinking and relating that empowers disciples and focuses on change, growth, and transformation." The book succeeds in defining, describing, and outlining how this can happen across the boundaries of faith traditions. This is a movement that holds promise for God's church. It is not something we should simply read and then put back on a shelf. It is a book we should read and then act upon.

—Ginger Barfield
Associate Dean
Lutheran Theological Southern Seminary

Preface

"These are the kinds of conversations we Christian disciples want to have all along. This is really what we should be doing anyway."

We were winding down the workshop in Disciple Development Coaching (**DDC**) when a minister spontaneously erupted with the statement above. It was one of those moments when a person has an epiphany or gains an insight, and it's all he can focus on in those moments. Throughout this training we could just see the wheels spinning for this minister. He asked questions, engaged the learning, and was trying to wrap his mind around coaching disciples as a form of Christian formation. When his light bulb came on, it did so with a flash. He spontaneously erupted with his insight. "Yes, this is what we have wanted to do in the Christian church all along: engage in substantive dialogue and conversations with each other about our callings, dreams, and challenges."

We have yearned for faith-laced relationships that provide a context for exploring our faith and life. We have needed support, encouragement, and even accountability to help us rise to the next level of our spiritual lives. And now, this minister was putting it together. **DDC** is a tool to facilitate this kind of relationship and conversation. It is an opportunity to help each other grow into more fully developed people who orient their lives around Jesus Christ. This minister discovered in **DDC** a format, structure, and activity for doing what he wanted to do in his ministry all along: intentionally developing disciples. But it was not always so.

In 2008, I (Mark) was invited to facilitate a lay leadership retreat for a mainline church. A third of the leadership team rotates on/off each year, so the retreat at the year's beginning is to set an agenda, gain inspiration, and start ministries.

I was delighted with this particular invitation, having coached the pastor for a while and learned what kind of leader he is. He is the founding pastor of this church, and the church had progressed through several developmental stages through its twelve years of existence. Now the pastor and the lay leaders recognized they could not "be or do church" as in the past. Due to size increases, no longer could the pastor be the primary disciple developer for every person in this congregation. No longer could the lay leaders operate as managers and not leaders or rely on the pastor to conduct all the leadership development with emerging leaders in the church.

Since coaching had been so helpful to this pastor, we decided to experiment with training the lay leadership in this concept. If the leaders could learn and apply coaching principals, then disciple development in this congregation could escalate.

In preparing for this retreat, I simply transferred many of the principals from coach training and practice to my presentation. I anticipated a great day and a half of learning, inspiration, and growth. About halfway into the retreat, the pastor and I used a break time to confer. "How's it going?" we asked. "Not good," we both answered. Quickly we refocused the retreat and restarted with a new agenda.

Later we debriefed what happened. The principals of professional coaching do have great promise for use in the church. However, the practice of coaching as it is designed for professional coaches cannot directly transfer to life in the church. The church's goals are similar, yet different. The church's context is unique. Professional coaches work by appointment, charge a fee, use professional forms, and have liability insurance. Life in the church is very different.

As you might guess, we traveled a long way between the first story and the second story above. Our current approach to coaching is the result of many starts and stops, of many learning experiences with clergy, church staff, and lay persons. Through the crucible of real-life experience, testing, and adjusting, we discovered and then refined our coaching process.

How do you decide on a name for a movement? Perhaps the best way is to allow the name to rise up from within the movement. This is how the name "Disciple Development Coaching" evolved. We did not sit down and think up a name, or narrow names down through conversation. Instead, this name found us. Let's deconstruct this name as a way to help you grasp the essence of the *DDC* movement.

Disciple

Following Christ's example in word, deed, and action

A disciple is so captivated by another that he wants to become like the other. He wants not only to learn the teachings of another but also to integrate and live out those teachings. A disciple is far more than a learner or admirer; a disciple wants to model life after the other. The Christian disciple orients all of her life around Jesus Christ. She wants to so internalize the life of Christ that Christ-like qualities, actions, and attitudes emerge from within. Student, learner, and follower are all good words, but they lack the comprehensive nature of discipleship.

Development
Growing, changing, transforming, and moving toward goals

Some development happens unintentionally. Physical growth in children is an unintentional process. Of course good nutrition, adequate rest, vigorous exercise, and a safe environment contribute to physical development, but the developmental process has a life of its own. Development of disciples is different. Although we grow spontaneously at times, intentionality is involved. God does not force God's self onto us, but God wants a relationship with us, as demonstrated through Christ's incarnation. To develop as disciples, Christ-followers must want and seek growth. This is our contribution to the spiritual journey.

Coaching
Facilitating growth in others through intentional conversations

We first used the coaching process with clergy and church staff but quickly recognized its usefulness for developing all God's people in their spiritual journeys. Building on the principle in Stephen Covey's *Seven Habits of Highly Effective People* that starting with the end goal in mind is a healthy practice, we direct our focus toward the end question of "What have you gained from this coaching conversation?"

After completing the following study on **DDC**, consider what you have gained. The book is organized into three parts: Part one provides the background, context, and foundation for and introduction to **DDC**. Part two describes the **DDC** model, along with examples and related practices. Part three focuses on the application of **DDC** to congregational life.

We believe that the Spirit of God is still moving among the people of God. Our prayer is that this **DDC** process will help open you and your congregation more fully to the Holy Spirit's movement in your journeys.

PART 1

Laying the Foundation

Brian McLaren's book, *The Story We Find Ourselves In*, tells about a pastor's journey to re-envision his ministry for postmodern people. McLaren's protagonist begins his journey by recognizing he must first understand the time and place in which he finds himself before he can minister effectively.

The story we find ourselves in is a given. We might wish and pray for a different time in history in which to serve, but this is the one given to us by God. As we attempt to describe this place, some characteristics are clear:

- *The world is rapidly changing.* The pace of change is exponentially faster now than for any other generation in human history. In addition, the change we encounter is discontinuous change. What has happened in the past does not necessarily give us clues as to what will happen in the future.

- *Distrust for organizations is on the rise.* Corporate corruption, financial failure, and government inefficiency cause many people to no longer trust the established institutions of our society. This distrust carries over to not-for-profit and service organizations watching their membership and contributions decline. Younger and middle-aged people are less interested in being part of professional, service, and fraternal organizations.

- *There is little toleration for meaningless activities.* People no longer want to give their time to meetings without purpose or clear outcomes. They are fed up with bureaucracy and "jumping through the hoops" to accomplish a goal.

- *The economy is unstable.* People are stressed by economic reverses and job losses. They have little loyalty to employers because they may be "downsized" tomorrow. As organizations grow flatter, many middle managers are losing their jobs and those who are left are asked to do more with less.

- *Spiritual sensitivity and hunger are on the rise.* As traditional supports disintegrate, people are asking questions about what is real, lasting, true, and significant. Often they seek answers in nontraditional ways.

• *There is a strong desire to make a difference.* Since many cultural foundations, institutions, and traditions no longer are secure, it is clear life is
transient and temporary. This situation drives people to evaluate what life
is all about. They want their lives to count for something and to make a
meaningful contribution to others.

• *The digital divide is growing.* In addition to racial and economic barriers, people now are divided into "haves" and "have nots" based on their
access to computers, digital devices, and the Internet.

• *The church continues forward.* Despite more than 2,000 years of challenging circumstances, we believe the church will continue its journey until it is consummated with Christ. In its current state in North
America, though, the organized church is showing signs of struggle.
Adaptive efforts by the church are underway, yet these are not keeping
up with the rate of change.

• *Weekly worship attendance is declining.* A generous estimate is that 20
percent of the United States population attends worship on any given
weekend, and this figure may reflect desire more than reality.[1]

• *An increasing number of Americans do not identify with any faith community.* These persons may soon surpass the adherents of the nation's
largest denominations. People are more "spiritual" and less "religious."[2]

• *The general population no longer holds clergy and congregations in high
esteem.* As the church moves more toward the periphery of culture, so
does the esteem of society for its leaders. The personal scandals and
financial excesses of some clergy contribute to this disaffection.

What does all this mean for Christian churches? ...

• *We must have clarity about our mission.* We must recover what it means
to be the people of God. The only mission we have is God's mission. We
are called out to do God's work even in a difficult and challenging time.

- *We must have a compelling story.* In an age when the Christian story is one among many, we must be able to clearly articulate not only the biblical story but also where our own stories intersect with it.

- *We must find ways to form disciples and involve them in significant service and ministry.* Christian disciples are hungry for ways to make a difference in the world, contributing their gifts to the mission of Christ.

The Unique Approach

I (Ircel) spent the majority of my ministry working with college students and their leaders. Working with young people as they transitioned into adulthood provided both challenges and opportunities. I made it a practice to meet individually each week with student leaders when I was a campus minister. One conversation with Dale, a pre-med student, provided a great insight for me.

I was talking with Dale about his spiritual development when he said to me, "How's your spiritual walk?" I must admit that my first response was, "Hey, I'm the spiritual leader here." I stopped for a minute before responding, however, and shared a bit with Dale about my own spiritual practices as well as my struggles in growing as a Christian disciple. I was reminded that day that every one of us, including myself, has an ongoing opportunity to grow as followers of Christ.

If disciple development is important to us, how do we go about doing this? One significant way to address the challenges to the twenty-first-century church is to find more effective ways to develop believers as Christian disciples. Equipped disciples not only will be growing in their own lives, but they also will be on mission for God in the world. We believe that coaching is one way to help believers grow as disciples.

For several years personal coaching has been recognized as an effective means of people development and leadership development. Coaching helps a person to clarify life purpose, values, and desired areas for growth and then to follow through by achieving personal growth goals. Coaching can assist a leader to be more effective in leading people and organizations. We have also come to recognize the value of coaching in disciple development.

Developing disciples is nothing new in the church. Since the time of Christ the church has used a number of methods to nurture believers in their growth as disciples. The Didache of the early church fathers, the catechisms of the Roman Catholic Church and the Protestant reformers, the disciplines of John Wesley, and the materials of the Navigators have all sought to lead people into a closer walk with God. *DDC* does not replace these traditional approaches but takes personal disciple development in a new direction. The goal is the same, but the process is very different.

All of these approaches take seriously the priesthood of the believer —every person is responsible before God for his or her spiritual and personal growth—and the importance of being involved in the community of faith called the church. In all cases, scripture plays a key role in the growth of the disciple. All embrace the understanding that Christian faith leads to Christian practice—orthodoxy leads to orthopraxy—and the second reinforces the first.

There are differences in the traditional approaches and *DDC*, however. Traditional discipleship processes are usually highly structured and sequential. The one who leads the process is a teacher or a mentor, and the "disciple" is led step by step by the "disciple maker." In the *DDC* process the believer identifies and develops her own structure with the assistance of a coach. The disciple discerns needs and formulates a plan to meet those needs. The coach's role is to provide clarity and accountability. This process presupposes some level of spiritual maturity on the part of the person being coached. In this approach the coach serves as a resource for the disciple as she pursues the path of discipleship.

In this book you will learn how the **DDC** process can be used as a means of personal and leadership development in a local congregation. You will also be introduced to ways to implement this process within the life of the congregation.

Growth in Christian discipleship happens in a climate of acceptance and accountability. The **DDC** process will help you to grow as a believer and to help others grow in their lives. Our primary goal is to "grow in the grace and knowledge of our Lord and Savior Jesus Christ" (2 Pet. 3:18a).

DDC is not the next new program promising to revolutionize your church or a curriculum-based educational program or a way to get disciples to volunteer for positions in the church organization. It is not preaching or teaching one-on-one or in groups or a theoretical approach learned in isolation from one's ministry context.

Rather, **DDC** is a way of thinking and relating that empowers disciples and focuses on change, growth, and transformation. It is an ongoing conversation with disciples in one's ministry context centered around building relationship, with our Christian faith as the foundation. It is a way to collaborate with God's redemptive and renewing work within each disciple.

DDC is an exciting way to do what Christian congregations already want to do: join God in developing disciples.

Biblical Basis and Theology

God has been working in the world from the beginning to guide, redeem, and transform individuals. We have the account of God's actions and humankind's response in the Bible. **DDC** is based on the teachings of scripture about how God works with each of us as believers. The following concepts are not exhaustive, but they provide an undergirding for this process of growing disciples.

Uniqueness of Each Person

Each person is unique. God has created each of us as an individual with special gifts and a personal calling. The Psalmist wrote, "I praise you because I am fearfully and wonderfully made; your works are wonderful, I know that full well" (Ps. 139:14, NIV).

Every person is precious to God and has the potential to serve God in a way no other person can. To that end we are "wired" in such a way that we can accomplish the calling God has given to us. Paul reminded his readers that "we have different gifts, according to the grace given us"

(Rom. 12:6a, NIV). God desires that we use those gifts to grow closer to God and to serve others.

As we coach others, we are aware that they are not like us. God has gifted them with abilities different from our own. The role of the coach in *DDC* is to help them discover and use the gifts God has given them. In so doing, each person has the opportunity to live out his or her uniqueness and calling.

Calling

Just as we are uniquely gifted, we are uniquely called. When Samuel was a boy serving the Lord, he heard the voice of God but did not understand what it was:

> The LORD called Samuel a third time, and Samuel got up and went to Eli and said, "Here I am; you called me." Then Eli realized that the LORD was calling the boy. So Eli told Samuel, "Go and lie down, and if he calls you, say, 'Speak, LORD, for your servant is listening.'" So Samuel went and lay down in his place. The LORD came and stood there, calling as at the other times, "Samuel! Samuel!" Then Samuel said, "Speak, for your servant is listening." (1 Sam. 3:8-10)

God has something special prepared for each believer to accomplish, but each of us must discover that calling. Calling is not something we inherit, receive, or manufacture; calling is something that unfolds as we develop the ability to discern it. *DDC* supports disciples as they identify their callings and live into them.

Transformation

Believers are always in the process of becoming. As the old saying goes, "I am not what I ought to be but, thank God, I am not what I was." Following Jesus is a lifelong journey of change. As we follow Jesus, we are transformed by the experiences of the journey. This requires a willingness to yield ourselves to him:

> I appeal to you therefore, brothers and sisters, by the mercies of God, to present your bodies as a living sacrifice, holy and acceptable to God, which is your spiritual worship. Do not be conformed to this world, but be transformed by the renewing of your minds, so that you may discern what the will of God is—what is good and acceptable and perfect. (Rom. 12:1-2)

DDC is about identifying and engaging transformative moments. In the coaching process we assist people as they become followers of Jesus at deeper, more significant levels.

Life Purpose

Life throws many things at us. Some things are clearly good, others are good but not a priority, and some things are just necessary. One of the challenges we each face is setting priorities and boundaries in order to give ourselves not just to the good but to the best. The Psalmist wrote, "Teach us to number our days aright, that we may gain a heart of wisdom" (Ps. 90:12, NIV).

Making decisions about how we will invest the life God has given to us is an ongoing task. We need a standard by which to measure the different expectations placed upon us by ourselves and others. Knowing our life purpose can help make those decisions. Being able to clearly state our life purpose can help us to be intentional and wise in the use of our time.

Consider the question, "If you knew tomorrow would be the last day of your life, how would you spend it?" Your answer to that question should give you clarity about your life purpose.

In *DDC* we have the opportunity to clarify the purpose of life for ourselves and then to make decisions appropriately.

Heart's Desire

When we follow Jesus, live into our callings, and are transformed, then our desires become God-shaped. Even our deepest longings become aligned with God's desires for this world. God's desires become our heart's desire. The Psalmist wrote: "Delight yourself in the LORD and he will give you the desires of your heart. Commit your way to the LORD; trust in him and he will do this" (Ps. 37:4-5, NIV).

In *DDC* the coach helps the disciple to identify his deepest yearnings, longings, and desires and to bring these into alignment with his life goals and then to live them out.

Priesthood of the Believer

Martin Luther began a revolution in the medieval church with his radical understanding of God's relational interest in us. Luther actually believed Jesus followers have direct access to God without mediation by a priest. This idea shocked his world, and we still struggle to apply it to our lives. *DDC* practices the doctrine of the priesthood of the believer by acknowledging that the Holy Spirit is in each disciple doing the work of transformation. Through Christ, every believer has been called to be a priest before God and a priest to others:

> [Y]ou also, like living stones, are being built into a spiritual house to be a holy priesthood, offering spiritual sacrifices acceptable to God through Jesus Christ. . . . But you are a chosen people, a royal priesthood, a holy nation, a people belonging to God, that you may declare the praises of him who called you out of darkness into his wonderful light." (1 Pet. 2:5, 9, NIV)

In one of our workshops, a pastor asked, "How will people in my church respond to this? They are used to coming to the pastor to receive direction and answers. How will they respond to the idea of finding their own answers?"

Believers do need biblical information and teaching, but they also need to learn how to make decisions for themselves. Jesus walked with his disciples, taught them and encouraged them, but when he was gone, they had to take up the mission he had given them. They had been fed; now it was their turn to feed. The process of discipleship results in a capable and responsible believer.

DDC helps disciples listen to the Holy Spirit's voice within them, believing the disciple is often the first one to hear from God about her journey, transformation, and calling.

Barnabas: The Patron Saint of Coaching

The Bible gives us the stories of a number of men and women and their journeys of faith. We read the unvarnished truth about these individuals —the good and the bad, the triumphs and the failures. One person is of particular interest to those who are involved in coaching: Barnabas, a leader in the first century church.

The man we know as Barnabas was originally named Joseph. He was a Levite from Cyprus who became part of the church in Jerusalem. Because of his unusual generosity, the apostles called him Barnabas, which means "son of encouragement" or "son of exhortation" (Acts 4:36-37). When Saul first appeared in Jerusalem after his conversion from persecutor to preacher, the members of the church were afraid of him. Barnabas became Saul's advocate, bringing him to the apostles and vouching for his conversion to the faith (Acts 9:26-27).

When church leaders in Jerusalem heard that the gospel was being preached to Gentiles in Antioch, they were concerned and sent Barnabas, a man they trusted, to investigate. Barnabas saw clear evidence of God at work in Antioch and became part of the Jesus movement there. He went to Tarsus to find Saul. Together they provided leadership to the growing Antioch for a year (Acts 11:22-26).

Led by the Spirit of God, the Antioch church set aside (ordained) Barnabas and Saul for a mission to other Gentile cities (Acts 13:1-3). On this first missionary journey Barnabas was the apparent leader, but he encouraged Saul (who became known as Paul on this trip) to exercise his considerable gifts. They established several churches in Asia Minor, but their success led to controversy with the church at Jerusalem about conditions to be imposed on Gentile converts. At the first church council, Barnabas and Paul spoke out for an unhindered gospel and were vindicated (Acts 15:12-23).

Paul and Barnabas began to make plans to revisit the churches they had established in Asia Minor, but they had a major dispute over taking John Mark with them. The young man had deserted them on the earlier journey, and Paul did not want Mark to be part of their group. As one might expect, Barnabas wanted to give him a second chance. The old partners disagreed so strongly that Paul chose another traveling companion and the two men parted ways (Acts 15:36-41).

Barnabas' confidence in Mark's potential seems to have been justified by later writings attributed to Paul. In Paul's letter to Philemon,

Mark is identified as one of Paul's fellow workers who sent greetings (Philem. 1:24). Paul wrote to the Colossians to receive Mark if he came to them (Col. 4:10). In his last letter to Timothy, he asked Timothy to bring Mark with him because Paul considered Mark a useful helper (2 Tim. 4:11). From this brief account, we can see that Barnabas exhibited the characteristics of a gifted Christian coach:

- He found joy in giving himself to others.
- He saw people through God's eyes—full of potential.
- He lived out the belief that God is at work in every person.
- He rejoiced when individuals joined God on mission in the world.
- He saw mistakes as learning opportunities—not terminal experiences.
- He exhibited unconditional positive regard—grace.

Barnabas provides us with a role model for the effective Christian coach, one who always looks for the best in others and helps them to achieve their goals. We are challenged to follow his example.

Implementation and Reflection Questions

1. What is the biggest challenge your church faces today? How can DDC address that challenge?
2. Review the theological concepts supporting coaching below. How do you perceive each of these in your own life?
   - uniqueness of each person
   - calling
   - transformation
   - heart's desire
   - priesthood of the believer
3. Who has been a "Barnabas" to you? For whom have you been a "Barnabas"? What was that like?

Notes

[1] C. Kirk Hadaway and P. L. Marler, "Did You Really Go to Church This Week?" *The Christian Century* (May 6, 1998), 472-75.

[2] "Trends among Christians in the U.S," http://www.religioustolerance.org/chr_tren.htm.

Seeking to Develop People

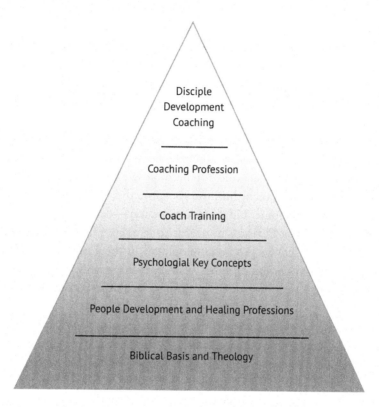

Disciple
Development
Coaching

Coaching Profession

Coach Training

Psychologial Key Concepts

People Development and Healing Professions

Biblical Basis and Theology

Six years ago I (Mark) was in a certification program, learning a particular form of training based on a personality inventory. Trainers from many backgrounds (coaches, professors, ministers, human resource professionals, medical providers, therapists) from all over the United States and Canada were involved in the training and discussions. Our interactions were fascinating as we wrapped our minds around how to train teams, departments, staffs, and other groups to communicate and function effectively—based on their personalities.

At one point in the training, someone asked an insightful question —one running through all our minds. Our trainer was describing his work with a large, multi-state engineering firm. None of us in the room were engineers by trade or training. The question was, "Do we have to be engineers to do this training with a company of engineers?" In other words, does a trainer (or coach) have to be from the same profession as those she is trying to help in order to be effective? Our trainer didn't even pause. "No, we are in the people-development business—not the engineering profession."

Our trainer's perspective was on target. Trainers and coaches are equipped to develop people, not provide expert consultation on the subject matter of one's profession or work. Through this discussion I couldn't help but think about the Christian movement. What business are we in? Quickly my mind sorted through the steps: making disciples (Great Commission), Christian formation, transformation, developing disciples.

A primary mandate for the church is to develop people. Part of our goal as God's church is to assist disciples as they grow into who they are in Christ and who they are called to become. We (the church) have been in the people-development business for more than 2,000 years. Yes, we do see people development in a very unique way—developing each other as disciples of Jesus Christ. Our goal is to live more fully and faithfully in the way of Jesus. So people development in the Christian church is not simply about communication, conflict management, or life balance —though these are all worthy. Our ultimate goal is to become more like Christ.

Knowing who we are and what we are about is very helpful when we begin working this out in real life. As the story above demonstrates, there are many people in our world providing "people development" services. To function well as ministers, church staff, Christian coaches, or lay people who learn to coach, we must understand enough about the various people-development services to serve people well.

People Development and the Helping Professions

Forty-five years ago my (Mark's) father served as a pastor of a fairly large church in a county seat town in eastern Kentucky. Years later I listened to him describe the experience. When it came to helping people develop or with problem resolution, my father was the local resource. Ministers in such communities functioned as pastor, priest, counselor, social worker, and teacher. Due to limited resources, ministers were called on to provide a vast array of services at the best level they could.

No longer is that true. Yes, there are still communities with limited resources. Largely, though, life is very different now. Fortunately there are many forms of people development available, provided by helping professionals with significant training. As they seek to make referrals and evaluate resources, ministers are often overwhelmed by the proliferation of helping professions and services, all claiming to have the answer to the world's ills or needs. Churches themselves may grow confused while considering how to connect people with resources for growth. As you may guess, we believe strongly in coaching as a helpful resource. At the same time our coaching experience informs us that coaching is not for every situation, need, or dilemma. Discernment, based on solid information, equips us to choose what service may be most helpful to ourselves and the disciples in our church community.

Counseling

After serving as a pastor and new church developer, my calling (Mark) evolved toward the field of counseling. I went back to school, earning a master's degree in counseling, followed by licensure in a couple of counseling disciplines. Walking with people through deep waters has been a special joy for me as I have served in pastoral and faith-based counseling centers. A significant number of professional coaches come out of the mental health professions. Given this and the similarities to counseling, insightful people often ask how coaching and counseling overlap. Are they the same? If they are different, how so?

Over the years my clinical caseload evolved to mostly couples (marital therapy) and ministers. As I worked with ministers in counseling, they progressed through their clinical issues or personal growth work and yet we continued doing counseling sessions. They needed an ongoing support structure. Looking back, I realize now that we had progressed into the gray area between counseling and coaching. I began to hear about the coaching movement, recognizing it as an emerging form of the helping profession.

My first official exposure to coaching came through reading. Pat Williams was a psychologist turned coach. In 2002 he and Deborah Davis wrote *Therapist as Life Coach*. When Williams came to our part of the country to do a workshop, I made it a point to be there. This is when my "aha" moments came. I realized this was what I had been doing with those ministers who had completed their therapy but were still coming for counseling. I was coaching them.

Do counselors do coaching, or do coaches do counseling? Since becoming a coach, there have been a few occasions where it became clear the coaching client was more of a counseling client. What did I do? Switch back to serving as a therapist? No, I referred the coaching client to a counselor when the need was apparent. I did not try to provide both services to the same person. Coaching and counseling are distinct activities—different forms of helping with different purposes and skills. Coaches and counselors have a high wall of separation between their practices. Yes, there is overlap, but the practices of coaching and counseling are essentially different.

How would a coach know when a disciple in coaching may need counseling? Sometimes the need becomes very clear, very fast. Some indicators are:

- Suicidal or homicidal ideation
- Clinical issues such as depression and anxiety interfering with the client's progress
- Painful historical experiences that repeatedly interrupt the coaching client's growth and advancement
- Thinking that appears disconnected from reality in a way that raises red flags for the coach

More often, the distinctions between coaching and counseling are more subtle, requiring a keen sense of one's limitations, coaching's purpose and place, and effective discernment. When the coach is torn about referring someone for counseling, the most effective action is to talk openly with the disciple about one's concern. Valuing transparency, authenticity, and integrity in the coaching relationship can lead to productive conversations about most anything.

I (Ircel) began coaching a person who was making a transition in vocation. As we worked together, this disciple became aware he was also dealing with some important family issues directly influencing his decisions about vocation. During one conversation I suggested to the client that perhaps some of the difficulties he was experiencing could be more effectively addressed if he and his wife engaged in marriage counseling. The client readily agreed and identified a professional counselor he and his wife could contact. The coaching connection continued but with a focus on the client's vocational concerns.

If the coach becomes aware that counseling is necessary, he can readily identify professionals for referral.

Consulting

Early in my (Mark's) coaching work, a minister in his first pastorate (let's call him Drew) called for coaching. I (Mark) was intrigued as Drew described his ministry setting: a small historical mainline congregation in a rural setting. As Drew and I established a coaching relationship, we explored his desire for coaching and his goals. This took more than one session since Drew was unclear about his goals. Through exploration and conversation, it became clear that Drew was not looking for learning, growth, or change for himself. Instead, Drew wanted the congregation to grow more open to change and then identify its vision for life and ministry together. Upon reflection, I realized Drew needed consulting.

"What will you be doing when you have reached your goals for our work together?" I asked.

Drew responded, "Helping this church live out its calling and vision."

I was curious how clear this church was on its calling and vision. "Not much," was the answer. The resulting coaching goal was connecting Drew with a visioning consultant. Drew wanted expertise from the coach, showing him how to do visioning work with his congregation. Although our organization does this kind of work, it is not coaching. Again, a referral was in order.

Consultants have expertise in certain activities, bringing their knowledge to bear on specific situations. Coaches are not necessarily experienced in the professions of their coaching clients. Consultants, on the other hand, should have experience or at least familiarity with the client's profession. Consultants inform, teach, and guide. Though coaches do some teaching, their primary method is to draw the expert out of the disciple. Consultants are hired for their expertise in a particular profession, situation, or process. Coaches are experts in assisting disciples to become who God is calling them to become.

Mentoring

Mentoring has its place, too. Mentors have something to teach others. Whatever age we are, all of us need mentor-type people around us, whether in an "official" or informal mentoring relationship. Some congregations organize "marriage mentors," pairings in which couples with more experience assist those having less experience to move toward a healthy marriage. Other congregations will pair more developed and mature disciples with newer disciples, helping them to learn the basics of the Christian faith. This is mentoring, not coaching.

More often, mentoring relationships are informal such as those revolving around coffee breaks and lunches. Mentors have more experience and more practical knowledge in some area of life.

For the last two years, three of us have met at the same restaurant one morning a week for breakfast. Both of the friends I meet there are older and have more ministry experience than I. We are friends and they are mentors, whether they think of themselves that way or not. We don't create an agenda for our breakfast gatherings. We simply share what's on our hearts and minds. Sometimes the conversation is deep and meaningful; sometimes it is trivial. Either way, simply being around mentor-type people and soaking in the conversation and wisdom is enriching. I learn much from these two mentoring friends.

Whether part of an official mentoring program or an informal relationship, mentoring involves a downward flow in the relationship. Mentors have more experience, knowledge, and wisdom than the mentees. The mentors have worked in the field—even if it's the "field" of life—and are willing to share their experience with less experienced persons. This kind of relationship is very helpful to disciples early in their faith journeys. When we are beginning to live in the way of Jesus, having someone to lean on as we walk is instrumental in starting well. Mentors fill this niche.

Spiritual Direction

Spiritual direction has been given and received as long as there have been spiritual seekers. Such practice has evolved to where one can now become a certified spiritual director. Though neither of us are trained spiritual directors, we know and work with many who are. We have observed the benefits of spiritual direction in the lives of colleagues, friends, acquaintances, and ourselves.

There are a few distinct differences as well as nuanced differences between coaching and spiritual direction. Spiritual direction tends to be accessed when people are looking for help in their spiritual lives and practice. People tend to seek out a spiritual director when struggling with a spiritually focused concern, problem, or desire (such as spiritual growth or discernment). Faith struggles, calling concerns, or spiritual crises may drive a person to spiritual direction. The motivation behind one's interest in entering spiritual direction is typically narrow in focus: spiritual.

Through our work and relationships with spiritual directors, we understand that spiritual direction can be helpful for broader life concerns than what we have identified here. At the same time, most people who seek spiritual direction tend to start from these motivations.

There are areas of overlap between spiritual direction and coaching. Coaching also is a great relationship for addressing spiritually focused questions. Many people seeking coaching start with these same questions. Coaching, though, is usually viewed as relating to a much broader scope of life. Many have developed a false dichotomy, describing parts of life as "spiritual" and other parts as not. It's all spiritual when we are living in Christ. People enter a coaching relationship with desires and concerns about many areas of life, all of them spiritual in nature.

Another distinction, it seems, is the desired outcome. Coaches help disciples make changes, grow, and take action. Insights and epiphanies often emerge from these outcomes, but they are not the goal of coaching. Spiritual direction tends to be more internally focused, seeking the insights and epiphanies. Later the disciple decides how to implement this learning into her life. Coaching includes and supports the implementation process.

The chart on pages 20 and 21 helps clarify similarities and differences between the helping professions. We realize we are painting with broad strokes, summarizing a profession in a few lines. Rather than providing a technical understanding of professions, this chart will help you identify the strengths of each profession or service as a tool for people development.

Key Psychological Concepts

As you can see from the previous discussion, coaching is different from other forms of people development. Although there are overlaps and connections between people development services, coaching has evolved to become a stand-alone professional discipline.

How did coaching develop? How did it come to be a distinct form of people development?

Like other forms of people development, coaching is a discipline emerging out of concepts and principles from many fields. Space does not allow us to provide a complete description of the history of the coaching movement. On the other hand, it is helpful to know there are some key concepts from psychology that have directly influenced the evolution of coaching.

	CONSULTING	MENTORING
Focus	Problem solving, action plans, specific problems	Transferring practical wisdom and skills to a less experienced person
Expertise	Consultants	Learned wisdom of mentor
Time orientation	Present	Past and present
Provider's role	Expert	Mentor has expertise, wisdom, and guidance to share
Relationship to "Why" question	Sometimes asks why	Not so much asking but instead communicates personal knowledge
Interest in problem's origins	Not interested in deep childhood issues	Not interested in deep childhood issues
Focal area	Specific project	Need of mentee
Who does the work?	Does specific pieces for clients	Mentee with direct guidance from mentor
Provider's methods	Finds the right plan as quickly and directly as possible	Teaches mentee what to do or not to do
Referring	Refer to other helping professionals as needed	Refer to professionals when needed

COACHING	SPIRITUAL DIRECTION	COUNSELING/THERAPY
Developing people through learning by doing, partnering between self-discovery and sustainable action	Listening for God's direction, gaining insights into one's spiritual journey	Understanding patterns of feeling, behavior, or thinking that maintain certain problems so they can be resolved
Expertise within client	Client's spiritual journey, with spiritual director as guide for understanding this journey	Expertise of therapist until client is strong enough to become the expert
Present and future	Past and present	Past
Active partner in eliciting dreams and calling of client, followed by designing the action	Background guide, facilitating interaction between client and God	Background guide, drawing direction from the client
Almost never asks why	Asks why as it relates to the spiritual journey	Often asks why
Not interested in deep childhood issues unless they impede progress, then refer	Identifies deep childhood issues that interfere with the spiritual journey	Focuses on deep childhood issues that complicate the present
Client's whole life	Relationship between client and God	Client's whole life
Client	Client does discerning with assistance	Client takes on work as therapy progresses
Has experimental spirit, sees failure as learning, looking for success	Listens for God's voice and watches for God's movement in client's journey	Focuses on insight and empowerment as soon as possible to relieve distress
Refer to other helping professionals as needed	Refer to other helping professionals as needed	Refer to other helping professionals as needed

Early psychology was primarily concerned with fixing what was wrong with people; focusing on pathology: "What makes people ill, mentally disturbed, unbalanced, and unhealthy?" This approach was natural, since psychology evolved from the medical field that, too, was pathology-oriented in its early days. Over time, psychologists and therapists and social science researchers became interested in another question: "What makes people mentally well, healthy, balanced, and content?" Resilience and happiness became key research concerns.

Positive psychology emerged as a concentration within the field of psychology. Researchers and practitioners in this concentration studied wellness, resilience, contentment, and other positive human attributes. Martin Seligman, former president of the American Psychological Association, was a strong contributor to positive psychology through his books *Authentic Happiness* (2002) and *Learned Optimism* (1990). Other researchers and practitioners grew interested in what helps families be well and do well. In *Strengthening Family Resilience* (1998), marriage and family therapist/professor Froma Walsh called attention to health, wellness, and resilience —attributes we desire in our lives rather than those we do not want.

As the field continued to evolve, brief therapy models emerged with a focus on solutions. Part of the impetus for this approach was managed care with its push for therapists to work more effectively and faster, thus saving insurance companies money. Though there are negatives to managed care, one positive outcome is that therapists had to identify quality outcomes focused on goal achievement for their counseling clients. As brief therapy models developed, one particular emphasis grew into a major new kind of counseling: Solution-focused Brief Therapy. Perhaps the best and most influential description of this model is found in Insoo Kim Berg's book, *A Solution-Focused Approach* (1994).

All three of these research and practice areas—positive psychology, resilience research, and solution-focused therapy—contribute to the practice of coaching. The following key concepts, mostly from solution-focused brief therapy, are incorporated into the field of coaching.

"Insanity is doing the same thing over and over again and expecting different results."

Some statements or quotes become permanently enshrined in popular culture. This one by Albert Einstein provides great insight into not only science but also human behavior. Now many people will quote this saying as the common (not clinical) definition for being "crazy." This perspective on insanity resonates so much with us because it accurately describes our tendencies when frustrated or failing. There are two corollaries to Einstein's statement, making it difficult to resist.

"If at first you don't succeed, try, try again."

You may have this saying echoing in your memory if you were raised during a certain period in our cultural history. The positive meaning behind it is that failure is not terminal and that trying again after failure will often lead to success. This perspective on life is valuable and empowers us to persevere and pursue progress.

Simultaneously, an insidious phrase has slipped into this saying over time, leading us to the definition of crazy above: "the same approach." Here's how this phrase has morphed over time: "If at first you don't succeed, try the same approach again and again." People have interpreted this well-meaning sage advice to mean we should take this round peg and just pummel it harder, trying to fit it into a square hole.

"If at first you don't succeed, try the same approach, but with much more vigor applied, again and again."

What do we tend to do when our first efforts are denied and we really want to achieve what is before us? Typically, we try the same approach again, but with much more energy and vigor behind it. If the nail does not go into the wood, hit the nail with the hammer harder. Apply more force. Or if that doesn't work, use a heavier hammer and swing it harder. Basically, we use the same approach but with more pressure and force applied. Sometimes this approach works. Sometimes simply using the same approach with more effort applied does the job, especially with simple basic challenges or tasks. When the challenge involves complexity or relationships or faith, however, rarely does this approach work.

Solution-focused therapy invites the client to consider alternative approaches to resolving the dilemma. Coaching involves thinking more broadly about challenges and concerns learned from the solution-focused approach. Don't waste more time pursuing the same approach even with more energy. Expand your view and discover there are many alternatives to approach most challenges before us.

"Find out what works and then do more of it."

After abandoning the same approach, which has not worked, we can move on to discover new approaches. Solution-focused therapists assist clients in determining what works in two ways.

First, identify when the solution is already present. In other words, when is the client practicing the solution already and the problem is not a problem? This kind of exploration directly helps one identify what works in relation to this particular concern or dilemma. When people or organizations learn to look through this lens, they find competence in their lives they did not know before.

In our congregational consulting work, we are often called to do conflict management. When we look through this perspective at congregations, we realize that churches resolve conflicts satisfactorily all the time. There are exceptions when experts are needed, yet the majority of the time churches solve their own problems. So, how do they do this? This is the question leading to strength and competency discovery. When the solution that is already present is identified, then do more of it.

Second, experiment with new potential solutions, discovering those that work. Perhaps it's time to change the old saying to, "If at first you don't succeed, try something new." Some therapeutic approaches include giving the client "homework" to do between sessions. These assignments are designed to help the client experiment with new activities to further their therapeutic work.

Beginning therapists often spend an inordinate amount of time trying to discern what homework assignment to give. The solution is that in some ways it doesn't matter. When the client is trying something new, the activity and action will lead the client to progress—often through trial and error. By trying something new, the client discovers what works. With this approach, one's perspective is broadened and expanded and solutions are discovered.

"Small change is generative."

How does change happen? Does it happen in an instant, or does it evolve through developmental steps? What about Christian conversion? Does it happen in an instant, or are we nurtured into faith over time?

Traditionally many of us have considered the Apostle Paul's Damascus Road conversion as an example of instantaneous conversion. In some respects that's an accurate understanding. In other ways, even in the limited information we have about Saul before becoming Paul, we can see how his faith journey evolved. When Stephen, one of the first deacons, was stoned, Saul was there to hold the stone-throwers' cloaks. He observed Stephen's grace under fire—literally. Surely observing Stephen's loving spirit, even in the face of death, impacted Saul.

Most dramatic conversions have the seeds of change growing in them long before conscious awareness happens. With this knowledge in mind, solution-focused therapists focus on helping clients bring small changes to their dilemmas by doing "homework" between sessions. Small change is generative: Once we get the ball rolling, it picks up momentum of its own. Getting started takes much energy, but once the ball is in motion, it tends to stay in motion. For example, I exert a lot of energy making myself sit down and write, but once I'm into the subject matter, it's hard to make myself stop.

"We are the experts on our life and our solutions."

Need someone to tell you what to do and how to run your life? That's easy. We can find people willing to do that most anywhere. The problem is that this approach rarely works or produces sustainable growth. Solution-focused therapists recognize that the solutions to one's dilemmas are best found within that person. The dynamics, nuances, and complexities of life are such that one person's solution cannot be blindly applied to every other person's life. Instead, solution-focused therapists work to help clients uncover their innate wisdom and perspective. More effective and sustainable solutions result. These may include the client seeking information or expertise from someone or somewhere, but the direction comes from the client. You will see this principle demonstrated in the coaching movement.

How much of a need do you have to direct others, instruct others, or generally give them their marching orders? If this is your tendency— and it is for many of us who want to help—then this will be a growing edge for you in your coaching training.

Remember the theology behind **DDC**. We believe the Holy Spirit is active in each disciple's life. We also believe each disciple is responsible before God with his or her own life. So we trust God and we trust disciples. This means our role as coaches is to help uncover, discover, and find God's direction for disciples. Our role is not to enter God's territory and tell people what to do.

Of course we are very sophisticated when we do take charge, disguising our telling as recommendations, suggestions, or advice, but it is still telling the disciple what to do. I often find myself saying to disciples I am coaching, "My goal as your coach is to help the expert within you rise up and become more active." We will revisit this often in *DDC* learning.

"A clear, positively stated goal is vital for progress."

Did you ever try to *not* think about something? Ever try to *not* do something? What happens? When our goal is to avoid, stop, or cease an activity—and our strategy is stated in the negative—we are unlikely to achieve that goal.

Weight-loss specialists learned this a long time ago. When a person wants to lose weight, weight-loss specialists immediately move the person to a new goal such as eating healthy foods or developing a healthy lifestyle or exercising. They know that when the strategy remains negatively focused—for example, "I won't eat ice cream before bedtime for the next two weeks"—the person is then fixated on the very food she wants to avoid.

Focusing on the object, activity, or concern in question keeps us highly engaged with the problem behavior. This psychological key concept from solution-focused therapy is almost directly transferred to coach training programs and approaches. We will find it in *DDC*. You will learn how to elicit the disciple's goal and then transform it into a workable, achievable, and positive goal. Simply moving through the process of goal identification and creation with disciples often generates great energy and hope. Disciples want to grow and change. Someone who can actually help them make progress is a godsend.

The Coaching Profession

The goal of *DDC* is both to develop disciples and to introduce a coaching culture into the church. Although *DDC* is not designed to develop professional coaches, it will be helpful for you to know how professional coaching has developed and the resources it provides for any type of coaching practice.

Executive coaching has been around for years. Leaders in large corporations learned early on that the complexities of their work life were overwhelming when managed alone. They also were smart enough to know that another set of eyes on their personal and professional functioning would help the company. They had the resources to hire coaches to help them along.

In more recent years, executive coaching has expanded to other areas of vocational life and then on to life in general. Now, life coaches are being trained and certified by the thousands around the world. This is an exciting time in the coaching movement. Coaching as a profession is still young and is characterized by creativity and energy. At the same time, a clear marker for a profession is in place in the development of coaching certification. Coaching is not as regulated as counseling, which requires state licensure. On the other hand, coaching is not completely unregulated, as with consulting. There are certification processes professional coaches have developed. They are willing to regulate themselves and embrace high professional standards for coaching.

The International Coach Federation (coachfederation.org), formed in 1995, is one of the largest professional groups and has more than 18,000 members. ICF provides the means for coaches to be certified in three categories: associate certified coach, professional certified coach, and master certified coach. Many local and regional coaching groups are affiliated with ICF. The ICF itself does not provide coach training; it certifies coaches instead. One can find certified training programs on the ICF website.

For those who want to work as professional coaches, we recommend they pursue coaching certification through the ICF. Charging a fee for coaching, working as a coach, publicizing oneself as a coach who makes a living through coaching—these are circumstances in which one is advised to pursue certification from the ICF. Some clergy, church staff, and laity will want to follow this route. Those who want to include coaching in their ministries and develop disciples more effectively in their own congregational context will typically pursue coach training such as the *DDC* model that addresses the specific needs of Christian formation and discipleship. *DDC*, rather than ICF certification, is structured to initiate a coaching movement in your congregation.

How developed must a profession be to have a precise definition? We don't know, but it's more developed than coaching is at this point. Perhaps the most conclusive definition of professional coaching can be found in that provided by the International Coach Federation:

> Professional coaching is an ongoing professional rela-
> tionship that helps people produce extraordinary results
> in their lives, careers, businesses, or organizations.
> Through the process of coaching, clients deepen their
> learning, improve their performance, and enhance their
> quality of life.

This definition describes coaching in the broadest possible terms.
Professional coaching is a very helpful people-development tool, growing
in activity and popularity. On the other hand, does this describe what we
are about in God's church? When it comes to the church's mission, it seems
we are focused more specifically than this definition conveys. Coaching
Christ followers includes many principles of professional coaching but is
focused differently.

Patrick Williams defines coaching as "a series of conversations aimed
at evoking the best" of one's clients and "helping them realize what they
want to change, improve, or add to their personal or professional life."[1]
Perhaps this definition moves us closer to a working understanding of what
we are about in DDC. Coaching is best done in the context of ongoing
relationships. Coaching is also conversational and interactive. The church
is a wonderful context for these kinds of relationships and conversations to
happen. We can form ongoing relationships focused on change, growth,
and improving life. Still this definition does not capture the primary focus
of coaching Christ followers. Two other definitions are helpful here, the
first from Joseph Umidi and the second from Dale Stoll:

> Coaches are change experts who help leaders take
> responsibility and act to maximize their own potential.[2]

> Mentoring is imparting to you what God has given me;
> coaching is drawing out of you what God has put into
> you.[3]

These definitions move us closer to our working definition.
Coaches are change experts, people who learn the principles and practices of change and can help others live them out. Coaches also know the
difference between mentoring and coaching, enlivened by a faith perspective. These are helpful insights into coaching disciples, but are not

comprehensive definitions. We now turn to our (Mark and Ircel) own working definition of *DDC*.

> Disciple Development Coaching is a focused collaborative relationship, resulting in the disciple living out his or her calling more fully.

DDC is not just casual conversation over coffee with no particular goal or purpose. *DDC* is a focused, intentional relationship. It involves goals, work, experimentation, prayer, thought, adjustments, and achievement. Our goal is for the disciple to rise up and live out his calling to the fullest extent possible. We will unpack the meaning of this *DDC* definition in the next chapter.

Implementation and Reflection Questions

1. Think back over your life. Are there people who have been mentors to you? Who were they? How would you describe your relationship with them? What did they help you learn?
2. Have you ever worked with a counselor or therapist? How would you describe that relationship? What issue did you address?
3. Have you contracted with a consultant at some point either as an individual or as part of an organization? What was the relationship like? What was the outcome?
4. Have you been coached previously either at work or as an individual? Who was your coach? What was the relationship like? What was the outcome?

Notes

[1] Patrick Williams, *Therapist as Life Coach: Transforming Your Practice* (W. W. Norton & Co., 2002).

[2] Tony Stoltzfus, *Leadership Coaching: The Disciplines, Skills, and Heart of a Christian Coach* (Book Surge Publishing, 2005), 7.

[3] Ibid.

Initiating the Coaching Conversation

We believe that not only does coaching have a place in the church but also that it can be an important part in helping every believer become the disciple God has called him or her to be. In order to do this, Christian leaders must learn and apply coaching skills in their own situations. In *Becoming a Coaching Leader*, Daniel Harkavy writes:

> As a coaching leader, you need to figure out how your product or service connects to some larger contribution. How does it help people to gain a higher quality of life? How does it enable them to operate more efficiently, contribute to their health, improve their outlook, or enrich their relationships? Regardless of your business, you must identify what need you're serving that helps to improve the world.[1]

Although Harkavy is not specifically writing for a Christian audience or for church leaders, his point is still applicable. How does what we are doing help others move further along in their relationship with God? What is the "value added" dimension of our work as lay or clergy leaders in a faith community?

One of the most important "services" we can provide to others is helping them grow in discipleship—becoming the women and men God is calling them to be. This will happen only with encouragement from a significant person in an individual's life. In *Missional Renaissance*, Reggie McNeal states, "Genuine spirituality lives and flourishes only in cultures and relationships of accountability."[2] Of course, our ultimate accountability is to God, but we can create and accept accountability structures in our lives that will help us to become more mature followers of God.

This is the primary emphasis of **DDC**. Every believer has a calling from God. Caring and trained coaches can help believers fulfill their unique mission within the Kingdom of God. This type of coaching empowers individuals, teams, and congregations to use their gifts, talents, and resources in effective and transformative ministry.

In these difficult times many of us are struggling. We need a new vision and a new focus for our lives. Coaching provides an opportunity to clarify our vision, discover our possibilities, and then to move forward with confidence. *DDC is a focused collaborative relationship, resulting in Christian disciples living out their calling more fully.*

The Mission of Coaching

Coaching disciples in the context of the Christian faith includes effective professional coaching principles and practices. Simultaneously, coaching disciples includes more than professional coaching principles and practices. We work from a theological and faith-based perspective. We are an extension of the church's disciple-forming ministry. The mission of coaching from a disciple-forming perspective is unique. Let's break down the definition of *DDC* above and harvest the meaning for coaching.

"Christian"

What makes people connections or relationships Christian? When the relationships are formed around the person of Jesus Christ, they are Christian. When the sustaining and enduring connector in the relationship is Jesus Christ, they are Christian. *DDC* is focused on advancing the spiritual journey of people who orient their lives around Jesus Christ.

"focused"

When relationships form in churches, they usually involve many aspects of our lives. We are not always talking about faith but more often are sharing our day-to-day lives in the context of our faith. *DDC* is more than casual conversation. *DDC* is focused conversation, spotlighting the growing edge of our discipleship. *DDC* coaches guide the conversation for the disciple's benefit.

"collaborative"

Remember the theological and psychological foundations of *DDC?* We believe God is active in each disciple's life. We believe the solutions and expertise are within the disciple. Therefore, we collaborate with the disciple and God to further the action. The *DDC* coach is not the expert from on high. Instead, the coach is a peer in the faith, helping the disciple grow and move forward. There is no room for a "holier than thou" approach in *DDC.*

"relationship"

How's your ability to form relationships? **DDC** builds on basic relationship skills. Though **DDC** includes a specific model with certain practices, one cannot simply "technique it." Rather, it is a model for coaching in the context of relationship. We will return to this insight repeatedly.

"resulting in and living out"

The learning theory Christian education programs in churches have used for years is the belief that knowledge directly leads to change and growth. With this learning theory, telling and teaching and preaching are the primary tools of choice. When one believes change and growth include many more kinds of learning, then we also focus on outcomes. **DDC** is interested in disciples putting into action their growth and learning so that real change happens. If the coaching only results in increased knowledge, then it's not Disciple Development Coaching.

"calling"

By now, most disciples have moved beyond the narrow definition of calling as only pertaining to vocational or professional ministers. Now we know that every disciple is called by God. We are all called to general spiritual realities, while we are all called to make specific contributions to God's mission. Every disciple is called and equipped to accomplish God's hopes and dreams for him or her. **DDC** is a tool for helping disciples discover, and then live out, this calling.

"more fully"

When are we finished living out our callings? Christian vocation lasts a lifetime and shifts over time. My (Mark's) calling now is to rear our children and be the best father I can be. At some point they won't need rearing anymore (in the traditional sense), but I can keep developing as a father until life is no more. All along the way there is room for me to live out that calling more fully. As disciples, we are always a work in progress. Our Christian vocations are ever evolving and ever active.

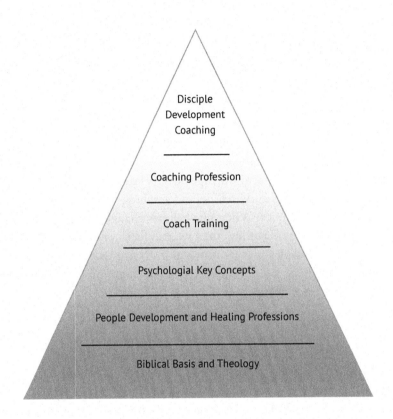

DDC evolved over time, combining insights from various per-spectives and professions. Our faith as disciples of Jesus Christ is the foundation. Involvement in people development and healing professions as applied disciplines gave our faith its practical expression. Learning psychological key concepts growing out of the health and wellness approaches focused us on positive growth and change. Professional coach training sharpened our understanding of the coaching profession and application of coaching principles and techniques. Experience in the field through coaching clergy, church staff, laity, and teams forced us to become creative around coaching disciples. This convergence of disci-plines, tempered with experience, produced DDC.

Now that you see how DDC has evolved and why a unique approach for coaching in the congregational setting is needed, we want to introduce you to the DDC conversation. This is the basic flow of DDC.

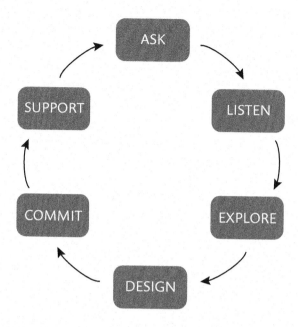

In one way, the **DDC** model is simple and easy to remember. In another way, it can appear overwhelming. This book is designed to help you begin using **DDC**. We will spend sufficient time with each component for you to understand and begin practicing each one. For each component we will learn its action, purpose, tools, and result. To introduce the model further, let's consider the basic action of each component.

- *Ask:* Action – Beginning the **DDC** conversation with a simple question, "What would you like to gain from our conversation?"
- *Listen:* Action – Listening to the words and meaning of this disciple's message; listening for the desires of the heart
- *Explore:* Action – Exploring alternatives or options before the disciple
- *Design:* Action – Identifying the action steps that lead to accomplishing the goal
- *Commit:* Action – Discerning readiness for action and making a commitment to take the fitting action
- *Support:* Action – Building the fitting level of support so that this disciple will accomplish this goal

Following is a sample of how **DDC** works. Jack is the coach and Bob is the disciple in this conversation. After reading through this coaching conversation, see if you can identify each step in the **DDC** model.

JACK: Bob, I've been thinking about our appointment since you called. What I remember is that you said you are experiencing some restlessness in your faith journey, especially around your service as a Sunday school teacher here. So, what would you like to gain from our conversation today?

BOB: Well, yes, that is what I told you when I called. And that is what I wanted to talk with you about. I'm just not sure anymore if I'm the best person to teach the class.

JACK: Hmm. So, suppose we spend some time with that. What do you want the outcome of our conversation to be for you?

BOB: Well, I really want to know if I should volunteer to teach again or to hand this off to someone else?

JACK: That's a pretty specific question. You want clarification of your calling as a Sunday school teacher for this next church year.

BOB: That's right.

JACK: How about telling me more about what brings this question up for you now?

BOB: I guess it's a couple things. One, I'm feeling this restlessness about teaching. I wonder if that means God wants me to do something different. And then another thing is that class participation is slacking off and I'm getting the feeling people are not connecting with how we do the class.

JACK: OK, it's more than one development that's making you rethink your calling to teach Sunday school. Help me understand the first thing you said . . . You are feeling restless?

BOB: Yes. When I get ready to prepare the lesson, my energy goes down and I end up putting it off and almost dread preparation. I used to not be that way.

JACK: Is what I'm hearing restlessness or more like dread?

BOB: Well, yes, it is more like dread. It's not like I have another option out there that God is leading me toward or like I am yearning to do something different.

JACK: It's more like things are not working as well in Sunday school and that is dampening your enthusiasm for teaching?

BOB: That's it. In the past I have really enjoyed teaching, and others tell me I have gifts for it, but it's just not working well right now.

JACK: How about if we explore some possibilities, if that's where you are?

BOB: OK. I really would like to teach, if it was going better.

JACK: So you would really like to teach, but not the way it's currently going. Without making any decisions about teaching right now, let's consider and explore that. Suppose you wanted to teach and you needed a way to improve the class experience. How would you begin?

BOB: Hmm. I'm not sure I can think of anything.

JACK: I'm glad to help with ideas if needed. But first, has anything run through your mind about this?

BOB: The thought has run through my mind of talking with the people in the class about this. I've held back because I don't want to put anyone on the spot.

JACK: It sounds like you are being sensitive and respectful of them. At the same time it sounds like you want their input, seeing that as valuable since they are class participants.

BOB: Yes. And I've thought of other ideas too, but that really seems like the place to begin.

JACK: Alright, so how could you get their input without putting anyone on the spot?

BOB: I guess I could call several class members and talk to them by phone, or I could do an anonymous survey or even email a few people. I'm not sure. We have been such a tight group, and we have made decisions as a group. I wish there was a way to do this as a group, a sensitive way.

JACK: Functioning as a group sounds important to you and this class. If you wanted to do this as a group, how might you do that—without having to commit to it right now?

BOB: Well, something we do often is break up into small groups to discuss questions and then come back together and report what we learned.

JACK: So they are used to doing that. What question or questions would you want them to discuss?

BOB: Maybe "What's working well about our Sunday school class?" and "What may we want to change?" If we discussed these questions, it wouldn't put anyone on the spot too much and it's a good way to explore the concerns. And, in fact, I could invite anyone who has additional thoughts to talk with me after the class. Or I could let them know I would be contacting each one of them for additional thoughts.

JACK: Wow! You are getting all kinds of ideas now. What does that mean to you?

BOB: I'm feeling more energetic and interested, which tells me this is the way I need to go.

JACK: How ready are you to commit to this pathway?

BOB: 95 percent. I want to pray about it first.

JACK: OK. How can I support you in this from here forward?

BOB: I would like to come back and let you know what I learn. Maybe you can help me think through the next step then. This has been really helpful.

JACK: I would be glad to do that. What Sunday will you be doing this with the class?

BOB: The 19th would work well, and then I could get together with you the following week.

JACK: That would work fine. How about if we have a prayer right now about this?

From this conversation you can begin to understand how **DDC** is a useful tool for facilitating growth opportunities for Christ followers. We are far enough into describing **DDC** now that readers may be asking:

• How would we use this in our congregation?
• When should we use **DDC**?
• What are the occasions or contexts wherein **DDC** is useful?

These are great questions. Toward the end of this book we will more fully describe how to begin a coaching movement in your congregation. There are several steps and processes to develop a coaching culture and mindset in your faith community. At this point let's briefly consider times, opportunities, and occasions where **DDC** will help your church move forward in missional ministry.

The Congregational Context

There are disciples in your congregation who are poised and ready to grow. Some of these disciples are very conscious of their readiness and even actively seeking ways to grow. Others are ready for transformation but don't know it yet. They are traveling and moving in their spiritual journeys but don't have the conscious awareness that they could move forward with specific assistance. Then there are other disciples in our congregations who have no idea the church could assist them in real-life personal transformation. They don't think this way since they have never been invited to do so.

All the disciples described above are great candidates for a defined *DDC* opportunity. Based on our experience, there are particular times in the lives of disciples when they are ready for *DDC*:

- When persons enter the life of the church and want to find their place of service
- When disciples express a desire to grow in their faith
- When disciples want to contribute to God's kingdom by serving but hey are unclear on direction, calling, and action
- When disciples reach out to the pastor, church staff, or trusted peer, asking for help with issues such as:
  −a major/minor decision
  −getting unstuck from a stuck place in their lives
  −feeling restless, bored, and stirred up
  −conflicted relationship(s)
  −a desire to learn new skills or grow in new ways
  −discernment of calling toward service
  −concern about the church and how it functions
  −a desire to change someone else

These are examples of real-life, real-time coaching opportunities in congregations. When you are trained and ready, then you are positioned to serve well to help others move forward in their spiritual journeys as they deal with challenges such as these.

Recognizing the usefulness of *DDC* to help during these significant moments in our lives is easy. On the other hand, visualizing how we might enter into *DDC* with disciples seems daunting. How do we wrap our minds around this endeavor? What are the handles we can pull to actually implement *DDC*? The following is a brief description of how congregations can integrate *DDC*.

Disciple development movement

When a person becomes a certified disciple development coach, she is equipped to train others in the congregation to do **DDC**. Through providing **DDC** classes, participants learn to coach others in the church. They are then trained **DDC** coaches. These coaches are ready to enter relationships with disciples who are ready for coaching, as described above. Then a congregation has a cadre of ready **DDC** coaches for ready disciples.

Focused equipping and empowering process for newcomers

"Assimilation" is the word congregations often use for integrating new members. This is an organizational word, focused on meeting the needs of the organized church. **DDC** is more concerned about developing disciples first, knowing this process will provide all that's needed for the organized church. So when newcomers enter your congregation, this is a perfect time for **DDC**. It can be used as part of your current process for newcomers. Even better, beginning with **DDC** will provide great direction for developing these new disciples plus connecting them with the ministries of your church in a personalized and focused way.

Training ministry teams, task forces, and committees

DDC provides many questions, activities, and coaching approaches that enhance team formation and team functioning. While it helps individuals accomplish goals, it can also help teams progress. From improving team functioning through more effective team meetings to identifying the team's working goals and moving ahead, **DDC** assists groups who work together toward a common goal.

Spontaneous and serendipitous coaching moments

You will be amazed how disciples who are ready to grow will find you when you are prepared to do **DDC**. They will do so for two reasons. First, you are trained and identified by the church as someone who can help. Second, you are ready to walk through the doors of ministry opening before you. In other words, you will have the eyes to see and the ears to hear when **DDC** is needed. Hallway and parking lot conversations become ministry opportunities for the disciple development coach.

Personal initiative

A significant difference between disciples who are coaching in a congregation and professional coaches is the connection they have with people who are ready for coaching. Right before the eyes of the disciple development coach are numerous disciples experiencing life, with all its joys and challenges, day by day. When one becomes a certified disciple development coach, recognized by the congregation as such, it is very fitting and appropriate to invite disciples into a coaching relationship when the need arises. Professional coaches do not typically have connection to disciples in congregations in this kind of seamless way. Disciple development coaches can, and should, initiate coaching invitations to ready disciples in the congregation.

Now we are ready to examine the steps of **DDC**. The next section describes each step, giving you opportunities to learn, practice, and integrate this model. First, we invite you to pause and consider your growing edges as a disciple of Jesus Christ. If you were invited into a **DDC** conversation right now, what would you want to be coached on? Identify a challenge, dilemma, hope, or dream that calls out to you for attention. Describe this growth opportunity the best you can. Carry the coaching item you have identified into your reading on each step. Use this real coaching item as a way to experiment with the steps of **DDC**.

Implementation and Reflection Questions

1. What does accountability mean to you? In what accountable relationships are you currently involved?
2. What is your definition of discipleship? Is discipleship expected of each believer, or is it an optional part of the Christian life?
3. Where would you like to apply coaching principles in your church or organization?

Notes

[1] Daniel Harkavy, *Becoming a Coaching Leader* (Nashville: Thomas Nelson, 2007), 87.

[2] Reggie McNeal, *Missional Renaissance* (San Francisco: Jossey-Bass, 2009), 104.

PART 2

Step 1: Ask

L ewis Carroll wrote, "If you don't know where you are going, any road will get you there." Former Secretary of State Henry Kissinger updated Carroll's statement in this way: "If you don't know where you are going, every road will get you nowhere." Or as attributed to Yogi Berra, "If you don't know where you are going, you might wind up someplace else."

The key idea in all of these statements is intentionality: Where are you going? What do you want to accomplish? Or applied to the coaching conversation, ask what the client or disciple wants to accomplish.

Begin the *DDC* conversation with a simple question, "What would you like to gain from our conversation?" Since the focus of coaching is the disciple, we begin where the disciple is. This is the first step in the coaching conversation and probably the simplest, but the response sets the direction of future sessions. At this point the coach wants to know the general hopes of the disciple for this particular conversation.

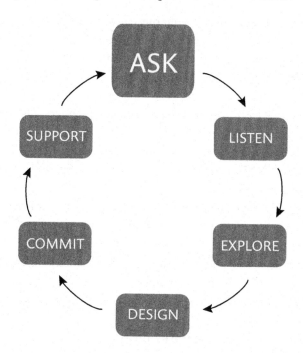

Action

In step one the coach begins to model the reality that the **DDC** coaching conversation is about the disciple and not the coach. When the coach asks what the disciple wants to gain from the coaching conversation, the coach is presenting the key to the whole **DDC** process. The coach's sole purpose is to help the disciple accomplish her goals.

Before asking "What would you like to gain from our conversation?" the coach may want to set the client at ease by engaging in interaction that will help to establish rapport or "break the ice." Some coaches refer to this interaction as "coming on board" activities.

As the coach and client converse about the weather, about one's day so far, or about something else minor, a climate of mutuality and interest is established. In this "warm up" time, the coach wants to avoid asking anything of substance that might distract from the coaching conversation to come or from the disciple's agenda. Monitor this time carefully and do not allow it to take more than five minutes of the coaching time.

As the coach seeks to discover what the client desires from the conversation, the question may be asked in a number of ways:

• What do you want to gain from our conversation today?
• What are you hoping for from our time together?
• What do you want the outcome of our time together to be?
• What do you want from our time today?

This action is basic, simple, direct, and open-ended. The question is meant to be very intentional, drawing a thoughtful response from the disciple. This query is more than asking "What's on your mind today?" The question is meant to begin moving the conversation in a positive, growth-oriented direction.

The key challenge for the coach is growing comfortable with this step. Do you feel awkward asking this question? If so, the reason may be that you are not comfortable with the client setting the agenda. Remember that the **DDC** conversation is about the disciple and not the coach. As a coach, you are helping someone else become what God intends for him to be. Your satisfaction comes from being part of that process of discovery.

There are clear reasons why the coach wants the client to set the agenda. Ask yourself these questions:

- Who might God speak to first and the most about this situation?
- Who has the most information about this issue, decision, or situation?
- Who is most affected by the outcome of this situation?
- Who has likely invested more time praying and thinking over this situation?
- Who has the most responsibility to take action in this situation?
- Who is most motivated to resolve the problem or further the action in this situation?

Of course, the answer to all of these questions is the disciple. The person with whom you are working is the expert about her life, gifts, and aspirations under the lordship of Christ.

Effective leaders and supervisors learn early that they cannot motivate another person. Each person chooses to act for his own reasons. Supervisors may threaten, demand, or require other persons to do something, but the latter will act responsibly only when they decide it is in their own best interest. Internal motivation is the most powerful motivation for change and growth.

As the coaching relationship and conversation develop, remember to keep the focus of this people-development process on the disciple.

Purpose

DDC is disciple driven, so the purpose of step one is to discover the disciple's agenda for this conversation and to help the disciple grow in his Christian life. Often it is challenging for beginning coaches to let go of their own agendas. On a daily basis, many of us are responsible for generating the agenda for interactions with people. As spouses, we have certain expectations of our significant other (whether voiced or not!). As parents, we keep our kids "on track" through various activities and decisions. As supervisors, we set up schedules and work our plans.

Coaching is not this kind of activity. The coach is the expert in process, while the disciple is the expert on the content—on what's important to this particular disciple. The coach provides the framework in which the disciple identifies needs, sets goals, and pursues them.

The first purpose of ASK is to discover what the disciple wants or needs from the coach; to begin learning about and assessing the disciple's goal.

If your typical style is to try to find solutions quickly, then this is a time to slow down. This is a way in which coaching differs from many forms of therapy. This is simply the first opportunity to learn in a general way what the disciple is looking for. In fact, this may be the first time the disciple has attempted to verbalize her goals. Further refinement will certainly be needed. The disciple's initial response will set the tone for a conversation. It will give the coach direction toward a goal or goals that will be articulated later in the discussion.

When the coach asks, "What do you want to gain from our conversation today?" the disciple knows we are getting down to business. This question moves the small talk to the side and invites the disciple into a working conversation. The wording of this question is clearly results- and outcome-oriented.

Coaching is concerned with action, movement, and growth. This is a way in which coaching differs from therapy. In the **DDC** conversation someone may state that his goal is to understand something or gain insight. Stopping there may be sufficient as a counseling goal, but a better coaching goal is to gain the insight and then use it in one's transformation process. The understanding and insight are part of the process of clarifying one's change or growth goal(s). Appropriate questions may include the following:

• How will gaining this insight play out in your life?
• What will you do as a result of this insight?

When the coach asks the first coaching question—"What do you want to gain from the conversation today?"—the disciple is invited into a process that has a specific outcome and result. This will not be a simple informal discussion but rather a movement-oriented, working conversation.

Tools

Most disciples will have some idea of what they want to gain through coaching. However, sometimes a person simply has a restlessness that needs exploring. The following two tools can help the disciple to begin clarifying what she needs from **DDC**.

In what we call "the view from 30,000 feet" we guide the disciple through a visualization exercise as follows:

You are standing at the base of a mountain. On the other side of the mountain is the goal you want to achieve or the future life you want to live. Close your eyes and visualize that desired goal or future. What does it look like? If you were to paint a picture of it, what would it look like?

Now let's jump on a helicopter and go up about 30,000 feet. Now you can see your desired goal or future life clearly. Below us is the mountain that separates you from your goal. What is the mountain made up of? People? Habits? Things you need to learn?

Now let's take the helicopter back down. Can you list those things that separate you from where you want to be?

Another tool we use is the "life balance wheel." In this approach we ask disciples to think about the various areas of their life depicted on this wheel, such as in the question below:

If "1" is at the very center and indicates "very dissatisfied" and "10" is at the outer edge and indicates "very satisfied," where are you currently in each area?

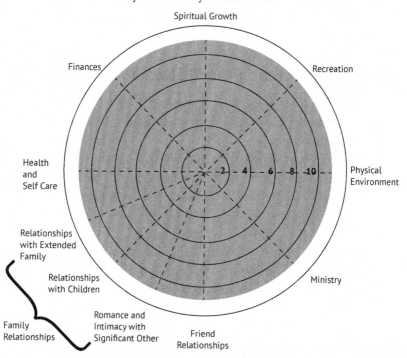

Our disciple development coaches use the life balance wheel frequently. Through experience we have learned to avoid certain assumptions about this activity. Identifying a low number does not automatically indicate a need or desire to raise that number. Identifying a high number in another area does not automatically indicate this area is where it should be.

There are many reasons and factors influencing why we may choose any particular number for any area on the life balance wheel. The insightful disciple developer asks open-ended questions of the disciple, inviting interpretation from the disciple's perspective. Used in this manner, the life balance wheel is a great tool to help disciples clarify what they need and want from coaching.

Result

As a result of asking and answering this first question, "What would you like to gain from our conversation?" the coach and disciple are now embarked on the road to accomplishing the disciple's goal. The goal(s) may not be fully articulated at this point, but the disciple understands that she will set the agenda for this entire process.

One of the gifts the coach gives to the disciple is the opportunity to state what she wants. The coach is creating space for the individual to think, dream, and plan how she can move toward God's calling. How often do we receive such a gift? This is something not only to treasure but also to use!

Implementation and Reflection Questions

1. Think again about the coaching item you identified at the end of the previous chapter. Do you have any fresh insights about it? Would you state it differently now?
2. Some coaches begin a coaching session with prayer, while others end the session with prayer. Some pray both times, and some don't formally pray in the session at all. How would you approach praying in coaching? How might it help? How might it hinder when not used well?
3. On a scale of 1-10, how comfortable are you with asking this first coaching question, "What would you like to gain from our conversation?" Consider some reasons for your level of discomfort with the question.

4. What are some settings where you could ask this type of question to bring focus to a situation and increase the likelihood of a satisfying outcome?
5. Match the statement in column 2 below with the activity to which it belongs in column 1.

COLUMN 1	COLUMN 2
Mentoring	"What would you like to gain from this conversation today?"
Disciple Development Coaching	"I want to share this knowledge with you so that you will know what I want you to know."
Spiritual Direction	"In our conversation today I want to share the wisdom I have gained in this area through experience."
Consulting	"After looking over your situation, here is what I recommend."
Teaching	"Let me explain to you a spiritual practice you may follow."

Step 2: Listen

According to psychiatrist Karl Menninger, "Listening is a magnetic and strange thing, a creative force. The friends who listen to us are the ones we move toward. When we are listened to, it creates us, makes us unfold and expand."

Listening is one of the simplest coaching activities—and one of the hardest. If you were asked to define listening, you could easily do so. Understanding and doing are two different activities, however. Despite our best intentions, there are always barriers to effective listening. Listening skillfully is very difficult.

One of my most frustrating experiences happened when I (Ircel) was doing my Doctor of Ministry degree work. Two other students and I scheduled a meeting with an administrator to ask him some questions about our programs. Rather than being attentive to us, he spent the entire meeting shuffling papers around his desk and reviewing his desk calendar. Although he assured us he could do more than one thing at a time, we left with the conviction that we had not been heard because he did not give us his attention. His actions and responses did not communicate to us that he was listening.

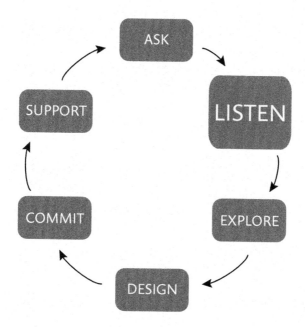

What kind of listener are you? When we listen well to disciples, our action influences the entire coaching conversation. Listening is a foundation for coaching. We can be less adept at some other steps and coaching can still be helpful, but if we fail to listen, the entire process is jeopardized. When we fail to listen, we undermine coaching's effectiveness.

Action

Our goal in step two is listening to both the words and the meaning of the disciple's message. In so doing, we help the disciple identify desires of the heart, those things that may be rarely mentioned to another person. We create a space where the disciple is really heard, perhaps for the first time.

What are we listening for when coaching disciples? Remember the definition: *Disciple development coaching is a focused, collaborative relationship resulting in the disciple living out his or her calling more fully.* Simply put, we are listening for that which helps disciples to achieve their goals. More specifically, remember that as a result of its biblical and theological basis, *DDC*:

- Supports disciples as they identify their callings and live into them more fully
- Identifies and engages transformative moments, assisting people as they become followers of Jesus at deeper and more significant levels
- Identifies our deepest yearnings, longings, and desires—holding them up to our faith for alignment and congruence, and then living them out
- Helps disciples listen to the Holy Spirit's voice within them, believing they are often the first ones to hear from God on their journey, transformation, and calling

Purpose

Why do we focus so much on listening in *DDC*? What are the purposes we hope to accomplish through effective listening? Consider the following goals:

Communicate unconditional acceptance.

We want to communicate *agape*, unmitigated acceptance of another person. The coach must demonstrate not only interest in the disciple's life and well-being but also a readiness to accept the person where he is in the spiritual journey. The coach models a non-judgmental attitude that encourages deeper reflection on the part of the disciple.

Connect at a deeper level.

We want to connect with the disciple at a deeper level, moving beyond the superficial pleasantries marking so much of our social interaction. When we show we are willing to listen, we go beyond the "everything is fine" comments of our usual hallway conversations with other believers.

Help the disciple gain perspective.

We want to help this disciple clarify his perspective. To help another person understand his personal needs and desires, we have to facilitate that person's conversation with himself. The coach encourages the "inner voice" of the disciple, reflecting back one's deepest concerns and desires.

Provide a safe place.

We want to create a non-judgmental and safe relationship with the disciple. The disciple should feel free to say things she has only said internally up to this point. The role of the coach is not to judge or impose values on the disciple, but to help her articulate deeply held struggles and aspirations.

Reiterate the disciple's responsibility.

We want to communicate again that this is the disciple's work. The disciple is presenting her life concerns, and the coach is facilitating this presentation.

As a result of this listening, the disciple experiences *agape* from being heard and understood. The relationship between the coach and the disciple is strengthened so that meaningful dialogue can be experienced. Effective listening provides insight for both the coach and disciple, with the disciple being energized to move on to the next step.

When the coach listens properly, both the coach and the disciple grow more focused. Allowing the disciple to tell stories unrelated to the coaching goal is not focused listening. Good questions from the coach keep the conversation focused. The coach is far from passive, being intentionally engaged in listening. In so doing, the coach helps the disciple determine what is germane to coaching.

The coach should recognize factors that interfere with listening attentively and deeply, for example:

- *Diagnosing*—When the coach adopts this perspective, she is considering what's wrong with this person rather than listening. The disciple is the best judge of his situation.
- *Evaluating and criticizing*—The coach is not a judge. The coach must listen and ask questions so that the disciple can evaluate his actions.
- *Strategizing or problem solving*—If the coach is considering how the concern or problem can be resolved instead of listening, she is assuming the responsibility that is the disciple's.
- *Distraction and daydreaming*—Listening is interactive, so the coach must avoid drifting off or paying attention to other things.
- *Exhaustion*—When the coach is overly tired, she is not ready to attend to the disciple.

Tools

The effective coach brings certain tools to the process of listening. Consider the following progression in the context of a face-to-face conversation:

1. The coach makes good eye contact with the person, showing that the disciple has his attention.
2. The coach cultivates an internal attitude of receptiveness and willingness to actively engage in this conversation.
3. The coach practices a disciplined quietness and a comfort with silence.
4. The coach focuses on the disciple rather than thinking about himself.
5. The coach displays receptive rather than guarded body language.

The effective coach is mindful of the disciple's focus, mindset, attitude, skills, capabilities, habits, practices, patterns, energy, and strengths as noted in the questions below:

- Is the client's focus sharp or fuzzy? Do you get the sense he knows what he wants?
- Is the disciple's attitude about the future positive or negative? Does he see problems or possibilities?
- Can the disciple learn new skills? Is he teachable?

- Are there things the disciple is capable of developing?
- Are the disciple's habits, practices, and patterns productive or nonproductive?
- Does the disciple display enough energy? If not, what is draining it? Strong emotion or reactions?
- What are the disciple's strengths?

Result

The result of effective listening on the part of the coach is the awareness on the part of the disciple that she is being heard. Listening requires a paradigm shift on the part of the coach. Those involved in ministry must move out of a proclamation mindset into a coaching mindset.

The proclamation approach involves discerning what God is doing and then sharing it with others for the purpose of persuading them to join God in God's work. The coaching approach draws out the disciple's discernment about what God is doing and then assists the disciple in living out God's calling in her life.

Implementation and Reflection Questions

1. Who would you identify as a poor listener? When you are around this person, you may be guarded with what you say or you may have given up on sharing much of anything. What makes this person a poor listener?
2. Who would you identify as a great listener? When you are around this person, you may find yourself sharing more than you expected and you are more relaxed and open. What makes this person a good listener?
3. Given what listening is and is not, how are you likely to get off track with your listening? Knowing yourself and your tendencies, what are you likely to do to sabotage your listening? Write down your answers so that you can clearly identify what parts of your listening need to improve.
4. Identify a person with whom you will practice unconditional listening. This may be your spouse, a child, or a co-worker. Practice active listening with this person. Ask questions rather than making comments. What did you learn from this exercise?
5. Think for a few minutes about your coaching item. Have you talked about it with someone? Did that person's listening help you to clarify your challenge?

Step 3: Explore

Jan's contractual position with a large corporation has financially sustained her family the last eighteen months, but the contract is completed (with no opportunity for renewal) next month. Her husband Ken has not been able to find a new position since the college where he taught downsized two years ago. Now, Jan is interviewing for an attractive position in a city located three hours from their home. Ken and Jan love their community. Their children are happy and flourishing in their schools, grandparents and other extended family live nearby, and they live in a pleasant and comfortable house. But they obviously need financial stability. Ken and Jan learn their church is training people to do coaching and ask if they can discuss their situation with a **DDC** coach. Their basic question is, "What is God's calling for us, given these circumstances?"

Zane has been a disciple of Christ for years, with consistent involvement in his church. Over the last nine months, Zane's spirituality has gone dry. He's still active in church, but the words of scripture are just words. His prayers seem to stop at the ceiling. Zane learned that you just completed the **DDC** training course and he wonders if you might help him move into a different place in his spiritual journey.

When she was called about serving as a deacon, Beth was surprised. She's only been a church member for three years and feels unqualified to serve. She loves Christ and this church but is unsure of her gifts and competency for this kind of serving position. Beth asks if you would meet her for coffee and help her think through this opportunity for service.

Josh lives next door to an interesting couple. They are extreme extroverts, inviting Josh over all the time for dinner and just to hang out. Early in this relationship this couple told Josh they both had terrible experiences in church and they don't want to hear about his church involvement, a request Josh honored. Lately though, they have been asking Josh questions about his church and even some theological questions. Josh feels uneasy talking this way with them, given their previous request. In addition, Josh is not sure how his congregation would react if this couple—along with their questions—became involved. Josh asks that you talk this through with him to help him resolve his dilemma and decide how he wants to approach this situation.

We could continue on, identifying innumerable situations, dilemmas, goals, and aspirations disciples bring to **DDC**. Sometimes disciples want help with discomfort- or pain-oriented challenges. Perhaps more often, disciples are looking for guidance or growth-related coaching. Either way, **DDC** is helpful because of its breadth as a helping model.

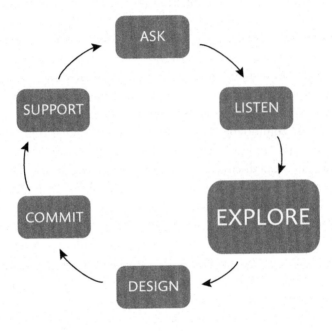

Action

The action in step three is generating and exploring alternatives and options with the disciple. Opening up, taking off the blinders, removing the filters—these are the images describing exploration. The disciple is invited into a safe space with the presence of God and the coach in order to explore a wider view of life and the particular challenge before this disciple. Through exploring, we broaden the view, thereby discovering alternative options for moving ahead.

Purpose

In the **DDC** model this exploration step serves several purposes. Disciples may expand their perspectives or discover additional alternatives for choosing a pathway or resolving a problem. The coach invites disciples to activate their creativity and intuition, making room for the Holy Spirit to work.

The Coach's Attitude

The coach's internal attitude directly influences how well the exploration step proceeds. In fact, the coach's approach to this step may be the primary influence on its effectiveness. When the coach is not ready for this step, he can shut the disciple down, leading to a stunted coaching conversation. When the coach is prepared for exploration, the client experiences new freedom to discover what God may have for him.

Disciples often describe this step as liberating. They may say things such as "No one has ever asked me those kinds of questions before" or "I didn't know I was even in a box until the coach began asking me those questions; then my creativity really rose to the surface." So what are the attitudes *DDC* coaches bring to exploration?

Prayer

To do exploration well, the coach must be spiritually centered. Being as connected with God as possible directly impacts the coach's ability to let go and accomplish this step. When we are "in Christ" we experience great freedom, giving greater freedom to others as we coach them. When we are not spiritually centered "in Christ," then we find ourselves clutching authority and controlling outcomes. The coach's faith journey is a vital part of effective *DDC*. Praying before, during, and after coaching is an integral part of the process. The Apostle Paul encourages us to pray without ceasing, and *DDC* is a perfect opportunity to practice this recommendation. Effective *DDC* coaches bring an attitude of prayer and spiritual receptivity to their work.

Reflection

The coach brings a reflective perspective, creating a relationship wherein reflection can grow and thrive. Reflection is the act of standing back and observing one's life and journey. People who are safe and relaxed can engage in reflection, while people who are anxious and scared cannot. To explore various options without undue pressure, the coach helps the disciple experience a safe and caring coaching relationship.

Curiosity rather than criticism

The coach cultivates a curious attitude about people, life, and God's ways in the world. Curiosity opens up people and situations. Coaches who practice curiosity as an attitude become great learners about life in general and about disciples in particular. When disciples experience the coach's curiosity about them and their options, their perspectives have room to expand. On the other hand, evaluation and judgment and course correction come together in criticism. Remember the action in this exploring step: generating and exploring alternatives and options before the disciple. Helpful criticism has a place in **DDC**, but not at this point.

Caring detachment

The coach practices caring detachment in reference to the disciple's alternatives and choices. As we listen to others and observe them working on a concern or challenge, most of us want to help. In our desire to help, we naturally evaluate options before the disciple. The coach's temptation then is to overtly or subtly influence the disciple to choose the option the coach believes is best. Instead, the coach must practice detachment. This is not an uncaring posture. Rather, it is caring enough to believe the disciple is in the best position to choose.

Visionary perspective

The coach brings out the visionary part of the disciple in the exploration step. Many coaches are visionary—seeing the potential in disciples, teams, task forces, or entire congregations. Often visionary coaches receive hints or clues about the greater potential before the disciple gains clarity. Using the visionary part of oneself in coaching is delicate. Visionary coaches can learn to draw out the vision of the disciple for becoming or doing. This is a great gift to the disciple, discovering someone who believes in her perhaps for the first time in her life. The danger for visionary coaches is in doing the visioning work for the disciple. In excitement the coach may take over the exploration, dreaming dreams for the disciple that she then does not recognize or own. Coaches must learn to use the skill of visioning with disciples, not be used by it.

Non-judgmental receptivity

The coach practices non-judgmental receptivity regarding the disciple's alternatives and choices, pursuing the deeper significance of each alternative. Some alternatives a disciple generates will appear ludicrous and ridiculous at first glance. The non-judgmental coach is receptive to these ideas, however, learning to drop his internal criticism of them as they are heard. Instead the coach may ask what the attraction is to this option or what's behind or below this option that draws the disciple.

I (Mark) recall a situation from my work as a therapist with a young boy who was generating solutions to his dilemma. He identified one solution as becoming the President of the United States of America. I was surprised, and internally discounting, of this idea. For some reason I had the sense to ask, "And what would you do when you became president?" The boy responded, "I would make my parents stop yelling at each other every evening and I would teach them to get along."

What insight! His "crazy" idea led to more actionable direction for the counseling process. Coaches with an attitude of non-judgmental receptivity continue pursuing the significance of disciples' hopes and dreams.

The internal attitudes noted above prevent less helpful and even harmful actions. When these helpful attitudes are not embraced and embodied, then the following actions may interfere or derail *DDC*:

• Evaluating alternatives or choices prematurely
• Judging or discounting the disciple-generated alternatives
• Going too fast, missing the opportunity to broaden the disciple's perspective
• Moving to problem solving rather than staying with exploration
• Limiting the disciple through "shoulds, oughts, or musts" (not based on their values)

The Coach's Questioning Method

In addition to internal attitudes, the coach's method of questioning can significantly influence the outcome of the exploration step. Questions are powerful. They guide conversation, elicit imaginative thinking, and open people to possibilities. Asking fitting questions is an art form. Designing and using helpful questions are primary skills for effective coaching. The two lists below illustrate the difference between unhelpful questions and helpful questions:

Unhelpful questions
- Questions that can be answered with a single word or phrase
- Questions that are actually the coach's wish for the disciple but disguised as an inquiry
- Questions that are evaluative or moving the disciple toward a choice
- Questions that discount one or more of the disciple's options or alternatives
- Questions that ask why and can sound judgmental and/or limit expansive thinking

Helpful questions
- What other alternatives have people who know you and love you suggested?
- If money and time were no longer limitations, what else might you do then?
- If you were to design the perfect solution to this dilemma, what would it look like?
- If you were suggesting some alternatives to a friend, what else would you suggest she consider?

Asking open-ended and generative questions such as those in the second list above will help the coach use the following exploration tools effectively.

Tools

The exploration step, more than others, uses a wide variety of tools for accomplishing the action. Before launching into these tools, remember the attitudinal prerequisites above. Using these tools without the attitudes in place will result in flat, ineffective, and simplistic **DDC**. With the necessary attitudes in place, disciple development coaches can use the tools below to advance the action with disciples.

Pray.
Christ invites us to ask, seek, and knock. We don't understand how prayer works, yet we have experienced its power to transform. Prayer is a great gift from God to the Christian community. At the same time, prayer is an under-utilized tool for growth and progress. With only a few questions about prayer, the coach can help the disciple discern, learn, and

identify options. Prayer is a great spiritual discipline and tool for expanding the exploration step. Here are some questions to employ prayer as a coaching tool:

- When you pray about this, what options come to your mind?
- If you are not praying about this, then what does that mean?
- What do you say to God when you pray about this?
- What do you hear from God when you pray about this?
- How will you pray about these options after our conversation today?
- What do you think God may be telling you about this right now?
- If you were to stop talking, grow quiet, and listen for God's whisper, what might you hear?

Examine scripture.

"I was really in a bleak place when we first started. The scripture with which I most resonated was Jesus on the cross saying, 'My God, my God, why have you forsaken me?' But now I'm in such a different place. I connect more with the man whose friends let him down through the roof and Jesus healed him. I'm taking up my mat and walking out of here with hope." This disciple reminded me (Mark) of the power of scripture to give us images, people, events, and an overarching story to define our lives. We as disciples enter into God's story and our story when we enter into the scriptures. *DDC* coaches use scripture to explore alternatives, gain understanding of the disciple's current state, and strengthen hope. Here are some questions to use.

- Which passages of scripture speak to you about this dilemma?
- With whom in the Bible do you resonate when you consider this dilemma? What does that mean to you?
- What passages or biblical stories might you want to avoid as you consider this dilemma? What could you learn from them?
- How much have you turned to scripture about this dilemma? What does this tell you?

Slow down the action.

Many of us conduct our lives as if we are afraid we won't get it all done before time is up. Disciples often come to coaching while moving at lightning speed. They are in a hurry to discover solutions and achieve their goals. The coach can slow down the action, inviting the disciple to take a deep breath, and live in trust that God will help him move ahead in the right timing. This awareness moves coaching from an emergency and crisis-oriented activity to a faith-based activity. The relief disciples express when this happens is satisfying.

Invite the disciple into imaginative space.

When life is not a crisis and when a caring relationship is in place, disciples can access their creativity. This is the experience created in the exploration step. The Holy Spirit is less constrained, and there is room for imagination—as with the following scenario:

> You are trying to choose between these two options. Suppose you let go of having to decide during this coaching conversation. What other options may present themselves if we simply let our imaginations run free with this situation?"

Allow curiosity without preference.

The Institute for Life Coach Training teaches a useful formula for achieving curiosity without preference. They call it the "equation for success," stated this way:

> Notice client's dilemma + Encourage exploration of all possibilities – Any opinions from the coach = Curiosity without preference.

Tolerate and welcome silence.

When you are not sure what to say or when people are not filling the space with conversation, rushing in with words to fill the silence is the typical tendency. *DDC* views natural silences in the coaching conversation as just that—natural. Even more, *DDC* coaches sometimes invite disciples into moments of silence. These may be used for listening to God's Spirit, listening to one's internal voice, or just resting from the struggle to discern. We invite you to view silence as a coaching tool.

Step back to see the bigger picture.

Video cameras have the ability to zoom in to see details and also to zoom out to see the bigger picture. Sometimes zooming out provides the perspective needed to gain perspective about a particular coaching item. Following are appropriate questions to pose:

• If you zoom out of this dilemma and take the larger view of your life, what do you see?
• How does this dilemma interact with the other components and dynamics of your life?
• How does this dilemma fit with the whole of your life?
• What does this larger view of your life tell you about this dilemma?"

Identify the parameters limiting perspective.

Some realities are not likely to change. Examples may include our basic personality, DNA, body structure, and core values. If we know these, acknowledge them, and accept them, we are free to move forward in life. On the other hand, disciples create limiting parameters, believing certain situations are "givens" when they are not. When the disciple is stuck, unable to consider alternatives, identifying the limiting parameters is a strong step. Then the disciple can decide how she wants to relate to this parameter. The good news is that many of these are imagined parameters when we consciously consider them with our coach.

Call on the wisdom of others.

I (Mark) can remember my first conversation about ministry as a vocation. A trusted mentor said, "You might want to think about going into the ministry. I see gifts in you that make me think vocational ministry may be God's calling for you." This observation was enough to raise the calling just below my consciousness to my awareness. Something within me resonated with this comment, saying "Yes!" I'm not unique in this experience. Often others in the community of faith see our gifts, talents, and callings before we do. *DDC* coaches invite disciples to ask for the input of trusted disciples about their journey. Many Christian faith traditions have encouraged collective faith community discernment for centuries.

Ask the "miracle question."

Early in the development of solution-focused therapy, creative practitioners developed the "miracle question" for inviting counseling clients into imaginative space:

> Suppose when you went to sleep tonight, a miracle happened. This dilemma was resolved while you were sleeping. When you woke up tomorrow, your life in this area was just as you hoped it would be. What would you do then?

Part of the beauty of the miracle question is its adaptability. I (Mark) find myself using it with individuals, families, teams, task forces, and entire congregations (changing it to fit the specific groups). The miracle question invites disciples to step out of their lives for a moment, using this miraculous frame for viewing their challenges. With this tool, many alternatives can be generated along with great enthusiasm and renewed energy.

Fast-forward time.

Through looking at possibilities of the future, coaches can invite disciples into imaginative space while focusing on action. Most people think in linear terms: If I do A, then B will follow, with C close behind. Paradoxically, sometimes we can elicit A if we go ahead and practice B or C. Doing the hoped-for solution will often work backwards in linear fashion to elicit prerequisites. An example of this tool would be this:

> Imagine clicking the fast-forward button on your life, going to the point where this challenge is met or dilemma is resolved. You are very pleased with its outcome. What will you be doing then?

Use metaphors and analogies.

DDC is action oriented. Identifying one's calling is only the beginning activity; then it's time to live it. Movement-oriented metaphors and analogies help disciples describe their journeys while also encouraging the next step. Often the Holy Spirit is described in scripture as wind, fire, or living water—all of which involve movement. This kind of perspective opens disciples to discovering alternatives that sedentary metaphors and analogies do not touch. Consider the following examples:

- Suppose you were hiking along and you came to a place where trails intersect. What would each of these trails look like?
- GPS devices sometimes give alternative routes, wherein you can choose the one you want. If that voice in the GPS was describing each of these routes, what would she say?

Result

Exploration is often invigorating and exciting for disciples. Before this step, disciples may believe no options or alternatives for their challenge exist. Through exploration they discover their vision is expanded, with broad vistas now stretching out before them. When one has been in a narrow and dark tunnel with limited choices or options, the experience of exploration with the coach is so welcomed. Discovering one has options when there appeared to be nowhere to turn is liberating. Now the disciple has alternatives.

Exploration moves the action forward. Coaching is not free-flowing conversation with no direction but rather a purposeful discussion focused on movement and growth. The exploration step in the process helps to identify various pathways and choices before the disciple, some of which the disciple may not be aware. Then, it readies the disciple for the next *DDC* step: designing.

Implementation and Reflection Questions

1. Consider your dilemma or choices again. Which of the tools for exploration are most helpful to you as you consider what to do? What does this tell you about how you are put together and about how you learn?
2. As you reflect on your Christian service or ministry over the last year, where do you see your energy and joy collecting? What does this tell you about yourself? Your strengths? Your calling? What does this tell you about who you are or who you are not?
3. What's a coach to do when the disciple gravitates toward a choice the coach believes will lead to failure? This choice is not immoral, unethical, or illegal but simply appears to be a poor choice that could lead the disciple to failure of some kind.

Step 4: Design

As invigorating as the visioning process can be, it's not the end of the story. At some point in the coaching the disciple identifies the pathway she intends to travel. Up until now, coaching has generated numerous potential pathways and multiple options. Coaching has been a broadening experience for the disciple. Now the disciple will begin narrowing, and eventually identifying, a particular option or alternative.

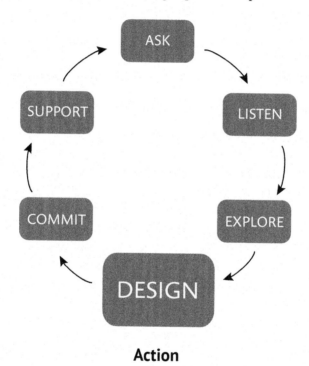

Action

The action in step four includes two activities: choosing and designing. First, the disciple must narrow and choose the goal. Second, the disciple and the coach design the first steps toward the goal.

Purpose

The design step gives the disciple clarity on the goal to pursue and then lends direction to the remainder of the coaching conversation. It also provides the first tangible action steps toward meeting the disciple's goal.

Tools

The design step is pivotal, especially for visionary persons. We have coached many visionary disciples who are thrilled with step three—generating options, developing visions, and articulating dreams. Since we coaches enjoy dreaming dreams with clients, we easily enter into exploration as well.

The challenge for visionary disciples and coaches is to move on. Choosing the course of action, not to mention implementing the goal, can be very challenging for visionary people. When disciples choose a pathway, identifying where they are going and how they will get there, everything grows more real. Eliminating options and saying goodbye to them can be painful for visionary people. Commitments to that pathway follow, and eventually one must actually step up and start moving. Sometimes we unconsciously delay the commitment and action by procrastinating in the visioning process. We invite you simply to be aware of the hesitancy or slight reluctance you may encounter from visionary disciples as you enter step four.

Before we move into the nuts and bolts of choosing the goal, consider these words about timing and pacing: By this point in the *DDC* process, coaching has a life of its own. Now, even more than before, it is time to trust the *DDC* process rather than forcing or coercing the action. Designing is fascinating from the pacing point of view. Sometimes identifying the future pathway is done quickly, requiring brief exchanges between coach and disciple. Through the exploration process of step three, some disciples experience "aha" moments or flashes of insight, identifying right then and there the goal they wish to pursue. When this happens, there is no need to spend time narrowing the options. The disciple has already accomplished this. Move on to designing the next steps through goal refinement. For other disciples, no fitting option arises during exploration, leading to this designing opportunity.

How then do we assist disciples in choosing their pathway ahead? What are the tools for choosing?

Review the options.

At this point the coach may lay out the options the disciple identified. Or better yet, the disciple lays out the options. The coach may say, "OK, let's review the options we have discussed. Would you review out loud for us?" If the disciple omits one or more options, the coach can ask if it/they should be included. The disciple may have already eliminated it/them. On the other hand, the disciple may be glad the coach remembered.

After identifying and reviewing the options, it is time to evaluate them for fit. This is simple when the disciple has already experienced the epiphany moment with a flash of insight about which option he wishes to pursue. When this is not the case, the disciple will often quickly eliminate options at the edges of center.

Two classic sets of questions can assist the disciple at this point. The first set helps the disciple identify which option draws her forward, while the second set helps her eliminate peripheral options.

• Which options drew you in?
• Which options called out to you?
• Which options do you find yourself leaning towards?
• Which option might have your name on it?

• Did any options immediately look unattractive to you?
• Do you find yourself being repelled by any of these options?
• Do any options eliminate themselves all on their own?

By either beginning with this first set of questions or the second—depending on your intuition in the moment—the disciple will narrow the list to one or just a few. Out of these remaining options, the coach invites the disciple to choose one for further consideration.

Assess the fit.

When considering God's calling for the next steps in life, how do you know? At times it's a growing awareness from deep inside. More often, knowing is more complex.

Circumstances, input from trusted people, knowledge, prayer, intuition, scripture—these are some sources of discernment when listening for God's direction. Or sometimes, one aspect of decision making becomes more important than another. Evaluating for fit from a variety of viewpoints helps the disciple identify which factors are most important related to this goal.

This tool involves trying on a particular option. This is a way to consider the option in depth, without having to make a commitment. In fact, making this assumption explicit maintains the freedom necessary to imagine doing this option and then assessing how it fits. The following are places to stand, pausing to consider an option from this point of view.

FAITH—The disciple can evaluate how congruent the primary option is with her spiritual journey by asking questions such as these:

• Does it fit into what God has been doing in my life?
• When looking back, does it help make sense of my experiences in the recent or distant past?
• When I pray about this option, what happens? Do I receive spiritual confirmation?
• Is there anything in this option that violates my spiritual values or understanding of scripture or God? If so, what does that mean?

FEELINGS—Psychologist Daniel Goleman's research tells us decisions that include our emotional intelligence will be far more fitting and effective. The disciple is wise to evaluate the chosen option based on how he feels about it, as noted in these coaching questions that appeal to right-brained intelligence:

• How do you feel when you try on this option?
• Does your energy go up or down when you try on this option?
• How important is it to you that this option feel right?

LOGIC—Thinking-oriented disciples will evaluate the reasonableness and soundness of the thinking behind this option, assisted by coaching questions such as the following that pull on left-brained intelligence:

• Does this option make sense to you?
• Is the logic of this option sound?
• Do you need any more information to understand this option?
• Do you see any holes in the logic behind this option?
• How important is it to you for this option to make sense?

CHALLENGES AND OBSTACLES—Believing that any choice will lead to progress without challenges or obstacles is wishful thinking. Even the most fitting choice of an option will involve change or movement. By considering the likely challenges and obstacles inherent in this choice of a primary option, one gains clarity whether this is the fitting goal to pursue.

- What are the challenges and obstacles you would encounter if you choose this option?
- How big are these obstacles to you?
- What size are these obstacles compared to the payoff of choosing this option?
- What "givens" exist in your life that could interfere with choosing this option?
- What does it mean to you that these challenges and obstacles are here?

VIABILITY—Given the big picture of his life, the disciple evaluates how this choice would fit. Issues to consider include:

- How much room do you have in your life for this option?
- What else might you need to change in order to do this option?
- What else in your life would be thrown off track if you choose this option?
- What do you want to do about the potential disruptions?

By reviewing the options and assessing the fit, the disciple has eliminated options and gravitated toward others. Through this point the disciple may have a clear choice. If so, she is ready to identify the goal and refine it. If not, she should follow these intermediary steps:

- Choose one option for now.
- Take a time-out for reflection.
- Recommend one option to the coach.
- Combine options into one.

Remember that choosing an option during a *DDC* conversation is not the final word. We have seen disciples return to another session having thrown out the agreed-upon option for a more fitting one. Other times, as the coach and disciple continue the process of working on an option, it becomes clear to the disciple this is not the preferable choice. When the coach embraces this attitude—no choice is irrevocable or terminal—then the disciple also embraces a more grace-filled approach to decision making.

Refine the goal.

From this point forward, we change our language from choices, options, or alternatives to goals. Now we are assisting the client toward her goal. Before we are off and running, refinement is typically needed in stating the goal and determining if it is an actionable goal.

One schema that has floated around the coaching world for years is the SMART goal approach. It remains a helpful tool for refining goals into actionable opportunities. When coaches first begin *DDC*, they often use this SMART goal schema in a direct and overt way. They may describe SMART goals, teaching the disciple what each letter means, followed by applying the schema to the disciple's goal. Later, as the SMART goal schema is more integrated, it becomes part of the natural flow of the coaching conversation. Using the word SMART as an acrostic, one can focus goals in such a way that they become actionable for the disciple.

SPECIFIC—Early in my (Mark) graduate training in counseling, the professor introduced a counseling approach that required the counselor to work with the client to identify a specific goal. The function of this specificity in the counseling field was to arrive at a goal that was actionable for clients who were stuck in unproductive emotional or mental sluggishness. When we grow specific about our goals, we are able to gain traction. They become actionable. Using the following questions while coaching disciples leads to specificity:

• Can you define more clearly what you want to accomplish?
• Can you sum up in one sentence what you want to accomplish?
• Would you be more specific about what you want to accomplish with this goal?

MEASURABLE—We tend to measure most everything we value. When we measure something, we give it priority. We need a way to inform ourselves about our progress or lack of it. When we identify the markers, then we know what we are working toward and we can gauge our progress. These questions reveal some of the logic behind the interest in making the goal measurable:

• How will you know when you have reached this goal?
• What will you be doing when you reach this goal?
• Can you quantify that outcome in some way?
• What will be the markers of your progress toward this goal?

ATTAINABLE—The most common derailer of attainability is articulating a goal that is beyond one's control. Typically disciples do this by identifying a goal that is dependent on someone else's volition, for example: "My goal is for my husband to begin attending worship with me." Though this is a worthy desire, it's not fully under this disciple's ability to implement. In this case the attainability question refines the goal to a more workable goal: "My goal is to invite my husband to the spring renewal service at church." The following questions can help the disciple move toward a more attainable goal.

- How much is the accomplishment of this goal under your control?
- Are there any "givens" in your life that would prevent you from reaching this goal?
- What is the likelihood that you can accomplish this goal in percentage terms?

RELEVANT—John Kotter's book, *A Sense of Urgency*, sits on my (Mark) shelf, reminding me that organizations need a sufficient sense of urgency in order to make substantive change. Teams, congregations, families, couples, and individuals are no different. I would like to rename this "relevant" aspect of SMART goals to "urgency," since this word seems to capture the essence of what's at stake (but SMAUT doesn't roll off the tongue well). By posing questions such as the following ones, the coach helps the disciple discern how important and urgent this goal is and can confirm or disconfirm this goal as the fitting one.

- In percentage terms, how much urgency do you feel about this goal?
- If you ignore this goal, what would be the result in your life?
- Is there anything else more important to focus on now?

TIME SPECIFIC—Often disciples will say to us, "I didn't expect you to ask when this would be done. That really helps me nail down when I'm going to do this. I usually leave out this step." Coaching is very action focused, so it makes sense that helping the disciple to identify the time when this goal will be enacted makes it more actionable. Relevant questions could include these:

- What's your estimate of when this goal will be accomplished?
- How long would it take to develop a long-term sustainable habit instead of merely making a surface change in this area?
- What's your schedule for taking the first step?

Identify the first steps.

The disciple's goal has been refined through the SMART goal schema. Now the disciple is ready to identify the first steps toward accomplishing his goal. The coach and disciple now engage in identifying that first step.

Identifying this first step may take thirty seconds or three entire coaching sessions. In other words, the goal drives the process. The relative size and weight of this goal drives this fourth step of designing. Separating goals into macro and micro goals helps us gain traction for designing the next step.

Macro goals involve the big picture of the disciple's life. These are long-term, highly involved goals, requiring significant time and attention to accomplish. Examples include:

- Discern God's calling for the next stage of my life.
- Discern if I'm called to enter vocational ministry.
- Discover the vocation to which God may be calling me.
- Identify my Ph.D. research area and then to complete my degree.
- Start and develop a non-profit, faith-based counseling center located on our church campus.
- Repair my relationship with my brother (they have been estranged for fifteen years).
- Improve or repair our marriage so that we can enjoy being around each other (may require a referral for marriage counseling).

Micro goals are focused in on a particular activity, circumstance, project, or relationship. They are short-term goals, requiring more immediate action in a very focused way. In order to take the first steps toward goal accomplishment, *DDC* coaches help the disciple break macro goals into micro goals. Examples include:

- Discern God's guidance about teaching on Wednesday evenings at church this fall.

- Choose the best seminary for me out of these three choices.
- Decide whether I'm called to specialize in heart surgery or heart research.
- Complete the introduction of my Ph.D. by next Friday.
- Find out if there is a need for a non-profit, faith-based counseling center in our community.
- Complete this work project by Thursday, and be in my right mind when it's done.
- Call my brother tomorrow and invite him for coffee at a time of his choosing (they relate frequently and had a minor hurt recently).
- Make a decision as a couple about participating in a marriage retreat next month.

So, what difference does it make whether the disciple's goal is macro or micro? Doesn't the coach do the same thing regardless? Yes and No. This is a place in coaching where the coach must be very clear about his role. The coach's role is to assist the disciple toward taking the next step. (If you were you a consultant, your role would be to design the process for taking all the steps between now and accomplishing the macro goal.)

The disciple may want to talk about that and give time and attention to it. Typically, coaches are more interested in creating movement and action. When a disciple really wants to design a longer-term process, from beginning to end, the coach may ask the disciple to work on this between coaching sessions. In the meantime, the coach and disciple will identify the next step that propels the action forward.

When the disciple is focused on a macro goal, the coach helps her break it down to actionable steps. Questions such as the following may help the disciple engage movement and action:

- What is your first step toward that goal?
- How will you get started?
- What will be your next action?

Typically, latter steps are so contingent on early steps that rarely can we plan far ahead with accuracy. Coaching accommodates for the systemic nature of life, recognizing that early action influences later actions in a myriad of ways.

You will remember Bob and Jack, our coach and disciple from the chapter titled "Initiating the Coaching Conversation." To determine what the coach did that was designing, re-read pages 36-39.

Design the action steps.

Remember that **DDC** is disciple-centered as opposed to coach-centered. The disciple does the bulk of the work in step four just as in other steps. Coaches use two tools during step four to help the disciple design the next step: listening and asking focused questions.

Asking "who-what-when-where-how" questions provides a helpful template for designing the next step with a disciple. When the action step meets the criteria in each of these pronouns, then the disciple is set up to accomplish this action step. The coach listens to the disciple's goal, helping to refine it through asking these questions.

WHAT?—The coach identifies with the disciple the next step. The coach may use questions such as these:

• To accomplish your goal, what's the next step?
• What clues do you have about where to begin?
• If you started working on this goal right now, what would you do first?
• What actions have been running through your mind as we have been talking?
• If we could fast-forward to the next time we are talking and you were telling me how pleased you were about what you had done about all this, what would you tell me?

WHO?—As with a goal, an action step is smart when it is attainable and under our control. When the action step involves the disciple doing and engaging, then it's doable. When the action step is focused on getting others to do something, then it's largely beyond the disciple's control. We are responsible for ourselves, not for managing the lives of others. On the other hand, we do have influence. So, a disciple can manage himself in a helpful way in relation to someone else. When we manage ourselves well, we have great influence. When we manage ourselves poorly, we can wreak havoc. Be sure to consider if this action step is under the disciple's control by asking who is involved.

How?—Now you know what the disciple will do and who will be involved in the doing. The next question is how this will get done. It may be as simple as 1-2-3, or it may take many complex steps. Remember that we don't have to know the entire process—just the next step. Breaking down the steps helps the disciple grow very specific about action. In addition, anticipated obstacles can be addressed while the disciple is with the coach.

When?—Identifying when the action step will be completed is one of the most helpful actions a coach can do. Sometimes coaches forget to include a timeline, removing a helpful motivator from the disciple. When the disciple states that next Tuesday at noon the action step will be done, then the disciple knows the parameters for this action. Identifying the timeline equips the disciples for success—accomplishing the action step.

Result

The disciple has an identified and refined goal along with the first action step(s) toward goal accomplishment. Now the disciple is ready to implement the steps, taking action toward goal achievement.

Implementation and Reflection Questions

1. Most of us, based on our personalities and life experience, tend to lead with one part of ourselves when it comes to decision making. Look again at the "trying on for fit" section above. As you make decisions about direction, which of these approaches comes most naturally to you? Is this the part of you that tends to lead when making decisions? Now, what does knowing this do for you?
2. Following are goals we have heard from disciples during their coaching process. Consider each goal, asking if this is a SMART goal. If not, experiment with changing it to a SMART goal.

- I want to increase the quality of my sermons over the next six months.
- In the next year I want to become a woman of God who is really in the Word and walking in the power of the Spirit.
- By January 15, I want to get my kids to spend 50 percent more time communicating with us parents than they do now.
- I want to set aside time each week to improve my guitar playing so that I can perform at the conference in June.

3. What has been your experience with setting goals? Has it been productive or nonproductive? Why?
4. What do you do when you encounter a barrier? Do you come up with alternatives? If so, how?

Step 5: Commit

At this point in **DDC** you have developed a substantive relationship with the disciple. You as a coach have asked about what's most important to this person and what's deep down in his heart. You have explored his sense of calling and made room for the Holy Spirit to speak into the disciple's life. You have invested yourself through listening intently for the hopes, dreams, and longings below his words. The disciple may have shared experiences, ambitions, and wishes he has not previously shared with anyone else. You have explored alternatives and pathways of choice, evaluating these choices for fit. The disciple has a goal (a SMART goal, no less) and knows the first step toward goal accomplishment. As far as he has come, two pivotal steps remain that dramatically influence what will happen from here.

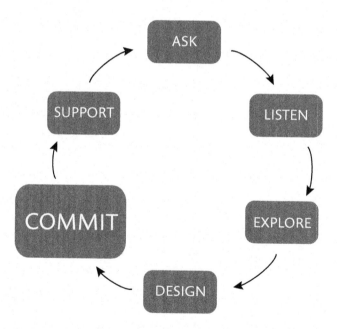

How many wonderfully crafted agreements about change never are enacted? At this point in **DDC**, the disciple has an action step waiting for her to get started. But does this disciple really want to pull the trigger? How ready is she for taking action? How important is this action to her? Enough to overcome the inevitable obstacles? What level of reluctance or hesitation remains within her? If these questions remain unspoken or ignored, the disciple is less likely to accomplish this action step.

Perceptive **DDC** coaches-in-training may ask, "What makes a coach so interested in commitment? Isn't **DDC** disciple driven? If so, what does it matter to the coach if the disciple commits to the action step or not?" In this chapter you will learn how commitment advances the action and why this is the coach's concern.

Significant progress has been made to this point in the process. Now the coach and disciple are moving toward the end of the coaching conversation in its first iteration. The disciple has shared what he wants, has described a goal or goals to work toward, and is invested in the outcome. The coach is in tune with his goal and his sense of God's guidance around this action. In this step the coach is simply assisting the disciple to do what the disciple has already determined to do. The coach does not own the goal. The coach facilitates the process for achieving the goal. The disciple does the work of moving toward the goal.

In this fifth step the coach is inviting the disciple to higher commitment; to doing what the disciple has determined to do. **DDC** remains true to its nature as disciple driven in step five.

Action

The action of step five is for the coach to help the disciple identify his readiness for action, making a commitment to the next step toward the goal.

Purpose

Some coaching models minimize attention to commitment levels or even ignore commitment entirely. There are times when coaches themselves forget or ignore step five of **DDC**. Our experience indicates that disciples who clarify their commitment levels and verbalize what they intend to do make more progress than others. There is simply something about committing to an action with another person as witness that propels us forward. The Christian tradition, with its Judaic antecedent, includes numerous covenants or agreements: God and Abraham, God and Moses, God and David, the marriage covenant, God and the church. This commit step may not rise to the level of covenant, yet it is an agreement on action.

Assist in clarifying readiness to take action.

Assuming the disciple is 100 percent ready to act is often a mistake. There are important reasons why disciples may not be ready to enact their next step. The ramifications for significant relationships may be large. The costs in other areas of life may cause hesitancy. Sometimes disciples simply do not believe they deserve to make this kind of progress; they don't believe life could be that good. Whatever the reason for the hesitancy, the reluctance to act itself requires attention in the coaching session.

Provide opportunity to raise the commitment level.

At this point we often use percentage questions such as the ones below, leading disciples to raised commitment levels. This step makes achievement more likely and is a way to anticipate roadblocks, turning them into open doors.

- On a percentage scale of 0-100, how ready are you to commit to accomplishing this action step?
- Is that percentage high enough for you to accomplish this action? If not, what holds you back and what do you want to do about that?

Allow opportunity to embrace or change the goal.

Providing the opportunity to commit to the course of action raises the stakes. There are times when the disciple decides she is not ready to commit to this action. If not, then there may be a preceding goal needing attention. Before accomplishing A, the disciple may first need to accomplish B. Through the process of tending to commitment levels, the disciple discovers another goal preceding the previously identified goal is really the first step. This may lead to goal revision.

Assist in clarifying the appropriateness of the goal.

Another purpose of step five is to clarify again if this is a fitting goal. Through this commitment conversation, the disciple may decide a different goal is more vital. We have seen disciples move to a completely different goal that is more relevant to their journey as a result of considering readiness to move ahead. Step five then serves as a safety net before launching off in a misdirected way.

Tools

The primary tool for facilitating step five is asking questions. The following are excellent questions for clarifying and intensifying commitment.

- On a scale from 0-10, how ready are you to commit to this action step?
- What priority level is taking this action for you?
- On a percentage scale of 0-100, how ready are you to accomplish this action?

When the disciple is not ready to take action, even after identifying the next step, then do the following:

Review the goal to see if it is really fitting.
Remember the purpose of this step is commitment—to give the disciple another opportunity to embrace or change his goal. This is a time to practice our faith. **DDC** is a discernment process. Through **DDC** we are better able to witness the unfolding journey of faith. By looking through this lens, we are not locked into the previously identified goal. Coaching, like life in general, is a very fluid process. This is the perfect time for the disciple to revisit his goal for clarification. The disciple may recycle through another round of exploration (step three) before moving on.

Refrain from pressing for commitment to this action step.
Early in coach development most of us feel an urgency to complete all six steps of the **DDC** model. We learn the model and imagine highly sequential and smooth coaching conversations where disciples are ready to take off toward their goals right away. Sometimes this happens. But our first priority as coaches is not to complete the model. Our first priority is to assist disciples in their faith journey. Releasing ourselves from the necessity to complete the model is vital for effective coaching. Instead of pressing the disciple for commitment, coaches maintain a caring detachment. Rather than criticizing the disciple (verbally or in our own thinking), we simply grow more curious. By looking through the curiosity frame, we communicate interest, caring, and openness to discovery. This approach rescues the coach from the slippery slope of criticism and control.

Refocus your attention and work on the hesitation or ambivalence.

The goal becomes exploring the hesitation around the action step. We devote whatever time is needed to exploring the hesitation and ambivalence. This is important work. This becomes the goal, and it can take more than one coaching conversation.

We are preparing you to coach when various contingencies arise but, most often, when the coach and disciple arrive at step five, the disciple is eager to commit to the action step. Given the six steps of the *DDC* process, step five often is completed the fastest. Don't get nervous when committing takes thirty seconds and is done! Because of the depth and significant process of steps one through four, disciples are often ready to move on when step five comes along.

Result

The disciple embraces the action step more fully, gaining momentum for action.

Implementation and Reflection Questions

1. As a coach, how will you respond if the disciple gets to this point and is not ready to commit?
2. Think back over the big commitments you have made in life— marriage, college selection, accepting or leaving a job. What motivated you to "make the leap"?
3. Consider again your coaching item you are advancing as you read. How ready are you to commit to your action step? If you are not ready, step back to observe what this means about your goal or your life circumstances.

Step 6: Support

In our work we often provide coaching groups for clergy, church staff, and other professionals. As people enter a group coaching experience, it is interesting to observe their expectations.

When they try to make sense of a coaching group, they draw on their experiences in other group settings. These include therapy groups, support groups, professional peer groups, Sunday school classes and other small group experiences in the church, and academic or continuing education classes.

As a result, participants are asking themselves how coaching compares to these other forms of helping. They often assume that coaching must be about healing, support, or learning information. Such assumptions are understandable, since we make sense of new experiences by comparing them to what we already know. In this case, all of these assumptions are faulty.

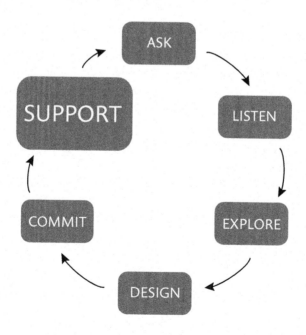

Although support is the goal of a support group or some forms of therapy, it is not the goal of coaching. Most disciples who experience coaching will describe it as very supportive, yet the goal of coaching is action. The idea is not simply to support the disciple but to move her to action toward a specific goal or life change. Supportive feelings and experiences are simply an enjoyable by-product of the coaching. In light of this, what does support mean when we are practicing **DDC**?

Action

Our goal in step six is for the coach to provide the support necessary for the disciple to accomplish the goal or, more immediately, the next action step. In doing this, the coach is not taking responsibility for the disciple's accomplishment of her goal. The disciple has developed the goal, identified the action steps, and is the responsible party for following through. The coach's role is to encourage the disciple in the successful completion of the action steps leading to the desired goal. Although the coach provides support in the way most useful for the disciple, the coach can also assist the disciple to develop internal and external support systems to assist in that pursuit.

Purpose

We make small changes on a daily basis, often without the support of others—for example, changing our hairstyle, losing two pounds, or reading a book we have put off finishing. We may want to share these small victories and changes with others so they can feel some of our joy or excitement, but we don't usually have external support to do these things. The situation is different when we are dealing with a significant change in our lives.

In **DDC**, disciples move into areas of change requiring concentrated effort and close connection with God's power. When change is this significant, we need others to support us in it. Our social nature influences us to accomplish goals more readily when others are cheering for us—or will be checking up on us! Real, lasting change is hard, but we don't have to do it alone.

Others have walked the path of change before us, and we can learn from them what is needed in the process. Significant change often requires a dependence on God. Most significant change happens within community and in accountable relationships. Since we know we need God and others for significant growth, let's be proactive about it! Support is built right into the **DDC** conversation. We use what we know to help disciples grow and move ahead.

By using what we know about the process of change and growth, the disciple is strengthened to complete the steps that will help him accomplish the desired goal.

The role of the coach at this step is to help the disciple build the appropriate level of support so the disciple will accomplish his goal. Since each of us is motivated in different ways, the type of support needed will be unique to the particular individual. Following are several options.

Assist the disciple to articulate what motivates her.

Since each of us is different, what encourages one person to accomplish a goal may discourage another. The coach might ask:

• The last time you were really successful in a task, how did you feel and what helped you to be successful?
• When you are discouraged, what bothers you most?

Help the disciple identify what could sabotage the action plan.

This is "worse case scenario" thinking, but the coach is helping the disciple to be realistic about potential obstacles. The coach might ask:

• What are potential roadblocks you may encounter as you start working on this action plan?
• Knowing your own lifestyle and potential temptations, how might you subtly sabotage this action plan without realizing it?

Ask the disciple to identify his support network and how to use it to carry out the action plan.

The coach may need to remind the disciple of spiritual resources along with the coach's own availability. Questions might include:

• Who is part of your support network?
• What can I do to support you as you accomplish this action plan?
• What do you want to ask God for to help you accomplish this plan?
• Who else would love to see you succeed at this action step? How could you enlist that person's support?

Provide some accountability to the disciple as she seeks to accomplish a goal.

Accountability provides energy for growth and change. Healthy accountability is not bullying, nagging, punishing, or forcing but encourages movement toward the goal. Remember that in coaching the only authority the coach has is that given to him by the disciple. To evaluate healthy accountability, the disciple should ask herself questions such as these:

• Does this give me life?
• Does this energize me?
• Do I want this to continue?

Help the disciple develop his accountability structures.

Examples could include the following:

• Use the coach.
  ("I will e-mail or text you when this action step is completed" or "When I am tempted, I will e-mail you and ask for support.")
• Commit to pray.
  ("I will spend two minutes in prayer before I engage in destructive activity around this goal.")
• Covenant with others to be a support team.
  ("I will share this action step with my wife, let her know when I plan to complete it, and give her permission to ask me about it after that date.")
• Covenant with another person who is undertaking a similar task
  ("Let's set up times when we'll check in with each other on our progress.")
• Build accountability into something you are already doing.
  (If you are part of a Bible study or prayer group, you might ask the group to pray with you about your desire to complete an action step).
• Utilize visible reminders.
  (Use a red sticky dot or a watch as a prayer reminder or a reminder to stop and think if a particular task has been completed.)
• Visualize the celebration.
  (The coach and disciple can envision how they will mark the disciple's accomplishments when they meet together again to discuss progress.)

Clarify the accountability agreement.

Ask questions such as these:

• What will you do? By what date will you do this?
• How will you know that you have been successful? How will I (the coach) know?

Tools

To help the disciple develop a support network and plan for appropriate rewards/reinforcement, the coach might present these two sets of challenges:

• Who are the people in your life that you trust the most? Write down their names.
• Think about your action steps or goals. Who is the person that would be most responsible in holding you accountable for that goal? Share your goal with that person, ask if he will hold you accountable, and agree upon a way you can do so (phone call, e-mail, etc.).

• What is your favorite thing in the world to do?
• Is there someone with whom you like to do that activity? Tell that person what you are trying to accomplish and make a date or appointment with her to do your favorite thing once you have accomplished your goal.

Result

Support is a valuable and necessary part of the coaching process. Each disciple can celebrate the fact that she is not alone in the process of change and growth. Others, including the coach, want to help the disciple to be successful in her task. Remember, too, that accountability is not punishment but simply another tool to move us along to success.

Implementation and Reflection Questions

1. List people in your life who energize you. List people who tend to drain your energy. How can you plan to spend more time with those people who energize you? How can people who energize you help you achieve your goals?
2. What motivates you? List things that help you get up in the morning and face the responsibilities of the day.
3. Who is accountable to you? For those persons who are accountable to you, how do you handle those relationships in a positive way?

PART 3

Starting a Coaching Movement

"These are the kinds of conversations we Christian disciples want to have all along. This is really what we should be doing anyway."

Remember this quote from early in this book? We have heard this insight expressed in various ways during *DDC* training. We conducted a pilot project on training disciples to coach peers in their congregation before *DDC* was a formalized initiative. Toward the end of one class I (Mark) asked, "What did you gain from our training session today?" The answers these disciples shared made it obvious that light bulbs were coming on for them as they considered how to help others in their congregation grow and change. One woman could hardly speak through her tears, simply from the peer coaching she was experiencing through the pilot project training program.

These Christian disciples were engaging in transformational conversations, with the coaching model providing the tools, structure, and opportunity. It's almost as if the coaching model gives us permission to talk with other disciples about what we hope to talk about in the first place. Most of us want to share our hopes, dreams, and God's promptings in our lives with other committed Christian disciples. This is part of what we hope church will be. However, the church often is not set up for transformational conversations. Deep, Christ-centered relationships are not encouraged. *DDC* provides the opportunity to be church in a transformational way.

Initial Steps

Why would we call *DDC* a "movement?" This sounds at best presumptuous, and at worst, grandiose.

As coaches, we keep learning and developing our skill levels. I (Mark) was in a continuing education seminar wherein the presenter was teaching new professional coaches how to capture clients. He described what we have observed, saying, "There are thousands of trained coaches who make nice websites and are skilled professionals . . . without any coaching clients. Marketing is really hard work."

This presenter advocates that professional coaches provide a complementary (free) coaching session to potential clients. Most professional coach training programs also suggest this approach when first beginning a coaching practice. The reason behind this suggestion: people understand coaching far better through experience than through description. Traditional classroom instruction in coaching is helpful, but it misses the power of coaching for transformation. Reading this book will help you understand coaching and also learn actionable skills. On the other hand, experiencing coaching will accelerate your understanding of coaching dramatically.

Movements begin when something invigorating is happening. Movements take a life of their own when energy flows, when experiences enliven, and when enthusiasm ripples. *DDC* is uniquely poised to go viral in congregations when disciples begin experiencing its transformational power.

So, how do movements begin? Sociologists, anthropologists, and activists invest enormous energy in researching the dynamics leading to social movements. Exploring this question is fascinating. Even so, we start with a more specific question: How do Christian movements begin and grow? Fortunately, physician Luke put pen to parchment, describing scenes from the early Christian movement. When reading the Book of Acts, we are struck with the simplicity (at least on the surface) with which Christianity spreads. There seems to be no detailed strategic ministry plan; no micro-level goals and objectives. Instead, the experience of Christian discipleship was so invigorating that people could not help but share it. No specific plan for growing the church was necessary. Informal processes sufficed.

At the same time there was great attention given to the purpose of Christianity; there was a clear macro-level mandate. Jesus gave the disciples and the church the commission to make disciples all across the world. This was big picture, expansive thinking. Jesus provided no detailed plan but gave a clear commission regarding intent: Go make disciples.

Since then the church has come a long way—and yet not far at all. Centuries have passed, giving the Christian movement a history. Like any movement involving people, our history is mixed with positives and negatives, advances and declines, authenticity and insincerity. We have come a long way in time and in methodology. During the last 2,000-plus years the Christian movement has been organized and institutionalized repeatedly. Most of our churches involve structure. They offer programs, ministry initiatives, and classes. Simultaneously, we have not come very far. We still gather around the primal story, the story of God's incarnation into this world through Jesus Christ.

What about now? How do we integrate **DDC** into congregations in a way that is consistent with both the biblical narrative and **DDC** principles? How do we take what we know about Christian movements and serve in ways consistent with this knowledge?

In the following chapters we will describe formal intentional activities for integrating **DDC** into your congregation, followed by informal intentional strategies. Formal activities can be replicated, offered by the congregation for the congregation (like a class). Informal activities occur as we go about being disciples day to day. How can informal activities, since they are spontaneous, be intentional? The early disciples were committed to making disciples (intentional) but without a strategic ministry plan (informal activities). So they naturally were ready to make disciples at any time, as informal spontaneous opportunities arose.

Just like the early Christian church, we continue the primary mandate or commission: to make disciples. This means relating to people wherever they are in their faith journeys and helping them take steps toward Christ.

One of the first questions participants in **DDC** training ask is about evangelism. Is **DDC** a program of evangelism? "No" is the technical response. Leading someone to conversion to Christ at some point in the process involves teaching. **DDC** is not a teaching tool; it is a maturing or formational tool for Christian disciples. Once a person becomes a Christ follower, **DDC** is extremely helpful for integrating and living out one's faith.

When we discuss making disciples in the context of the **DDC** conversation, we are describing the Christian formation process. We start wherever the Christian disciple is in his journey and then assist him in growth from there forward. Making disciples means contributing to the maturing process, growth journey, and development of Christ followers into more faithful Christ followers. This is the purpose of **DDC**, as outlined earlier in the following flow:

• Develop disciples (macro goal)
• Coach every ready disciple in every ready congregation (micro goal)
• Teach Disciple Development Coaching courses in your congregation (methodology)

Most congregations are involved in developing disciples. Worship, evangelism, disciple care, missional ministries, learning experiences, community building—all these activities contribute to disciple development. Now churches can also use the *DDC* tool to help accomplish their disciple development mission.

After reading this book you will be familiar with the basic *DDC* conversation model. We hope you are using what you have learned already with yourself and other disciples. There is no reason to hold back from entering into transformational conversations with those who are ready and open. Begin using *DDC* in every opportunity that presents itself. We trust God to lead you into meaningful and rich *DDC* conversations as you and others are ready and available.

At the same time we hope that many readers will take the next step in *DDC* training so they can teach *DDC* classes in their congregations. This is the primary method for integrating *DDC* into your ministry context. Certified *DDC* coaches can teach as many classes as possible with the goal of training as many disciples in a particular congregation as possible. Through the course, disciples learn the *DDC* approach and conversation, along with practice in a safe setting. Participants coach a "buddy" during the course, gaining real *DDC* experience. After the course, these disciples are equipped to coach others in the congregation.

Certification

Training is needed to teach a *DDC* course in a congregation. This is where *DDC* certification is helpful. Reading this book equips readers to begin using *DDC* informally, yet it does not suffice for training others to use *DDC*. Participants in *DDC* certification will reap added benefits such as the following:

• Learn the *DDC* model and become competent to coach disciples
• Gain hands-on experience in the *DDC* course and practicum through buddy coaching
• Coach disciples with oversight from a *DDC* trainer
• Learn how to train others through teaching classes
• Gain access to class materials for training *DDC* coaches

Our goal is to equip coaches to train disciples in congregations to coach one another using the **DDC** model. Since we are a limited resource, we cannot do this training ourselves. Instead, we are training clergy, church staff, and lay persons in the **DDC** model so they can bring **DDC** to their contexts.

To accomplish this goal, we invite disciples to consider **DDC** certification, which includes the following steps:

*1. Complete the **DDC** course.*

During twenty hours of class time we engage in learning activities with a wide variety of learning styles. In addition to learning information, participants gain real time experience in using the model with peers in the course. Examples, demonstrations, and discussions permeate this experience.

2. Participate in a disciple development practicum.

During this six-month practicum, participants coach disciples in their ministry context. Monthly teleconference classes support this **DDC** coaching with oversight from a **DDC** trainer. In addition, participants are paired with a "buddy" coach for practicing the model. Toward the end of this practicum, participants demonstrate their proficiency using the **DDC** model.

3. Teach disciple development classes.

At this point, participants become Certified Disciple Development Coaches. This competency-based certification equips them to train other disciples in their congregation to use the model. Certified **DDC** coaches can order our training materials for teaching these classes. Participants in the class will coach a "buddy" in the class, learning the **DDC** model by doing. After the class is completed, many disciples will continue coaching their buddies. Congregations are then equipped with a cadre of **DDC** coaches who can coach others who are ready to live out their callings at a higher level. Certified **DDC** coaches can replicate these classes as often as needed. Through the **DDC** certification process, participants learn how to recruit other participants and teach effective **DDC** classes.

Implementation and Reflection Questions

1. Reflect on your congregation as a "disciple-developing congregation." How much does this phrase reflect the priorities of your congregation?
2. Who are the disciples in your congregation who may be ready to be trained as coaches? These are people who genuinely care about others, are able to listen, and want others to flourish in their life journeys.
3. Could you see yourself becoming a Certified Disciple Development Coach? When considering this, what feelings and thoughts rise up in you? Might you want to make this a matter of prayer?

Becoming a Disciple-developing Congregation

They were a small church. This is how they first identified themselves when they called about a visioning process. One of the first questions I (Mark) asked as we began our discernment work was what "small" meant to them. They answered by describing deficits. "We are not big, we don't offer many programs, we don't have a lot of children and youth, we only do one style of worship . . ." Small, to them, meant less than. This congregation was suffering from low self-esteem.

The visioning work with this congregation involved mining for the members' assets, gifts, themes, and strengths. Through much conversation they discovered a high percentage of their members were serving in their community. An older gentleman volunteered at the Veterans Administration hospital three days a week, walking the hallways and greeting the veterans. He smiled, listened, cared, and was a welcoming presence. A group of their youth and children conducted an informal soccer camp in their neighborhood each summer. This camp included a brief devotional and prayer to start the day. A woman in this church had a gift for gardening. She invested herself in beautifying the church campus but also in teaching her neighbors to grow healthy plants. I could go on. All of these disciples saw their service as part of their Christian calling. They served in the name of Christ and spoke about Christ as the opportunities arose.

At first this church discounted these stories, thinking they did not "count" because they were not official church ministries. But the more they talked and shared and then really listened, the more they realized these disciples were being the hands and feet of Christ in their community. There was no way to program this as a church function. Instead, the church's role was to incubate this spirit. Each one of these people described the spiritual nurture of their church as what gave them the fuel for serving. This small church decided its role was to be an incubator of ministry—whether provided through an official church function or not. The church folk recognized they were a disciple-developing community of faith. Small no longer had relevance to their self-image as a congregation. They were disciple developers.

In the previous chapter we considered how to start a congregational movement in *DDC*. Teaching classes and coaching disciples are very tangible ways to initiate this movement. But becoming a disciple-developing congregation involves another level of integration. Teaching classes and coaching disciples can initiate this movement, but integration must follow. The congregation described above adopted the image of "incubator" for its ministry. The members focused on activities, processes, and endeavors that grew disciples of Jesus Christ. When they focused on incubating, they found new life springing up in many ways. One obvious sign was the multiple ministries of individual disciples in their community.

This brings us back to the important question of, "What is the essential mission of the Christian church?" Though the answer is multifaceted, developing disciples is central. What other organization is focused on developing disciples of Jesus Christ? Perhaps there are parachurch organizations specializing in aspects of the disciple-developing mission, but the church is uniquely tasked with the responsibility for disciple development.

Where do we begin when we want to become a disciple-developing congregation—not in only what we do but also as a way of life?

Pastoral Priority

Early in ministry, pastors and church staff move through a formational process. Certainly we have formal processes for becoming a minister including ordination, but does the act of ordination on a particular day make one a fully formed pastoral minister? Technically, yes. Formationally, developmentally, and practically—no.

For those who are married, we can remember our wedding day as the day we were "officially" married. With minimal reflection we are aware we were married somewhat before the ceremony and we were also becoming married long after the ceremony was a memory.

Becoming a minister is a growth process over time, just like all the other significant transformational processes of our lives. Therefore, ministers must develop their "philosophy" of ministry through living and serving in their calling. The following questions may help them formulate this concept:

- What is the mission of the church?
- What is essential to the church's ministry?
- How do we spend our time and resources?
- What is at the core of church life?
- What must we do?

Most clergy and church staff include making and developing disciples in their answers to these questions. Through our coaching work we are exposed to the thinking, perspectives, and hopes of many clergy from various Christian denominations. Living a healthy and effective pastoral life is complex and challenging. Ministers struggle with meeting institutional needs while maintaining a focus on disciple development. Sometimes managing the organization overwhelms the purpose for the organization. Calling ourselves back to our primary mission of developing disciples is a necessary daily discipline.

Pastors who are convinced developing disciples is at the core of their congregation's calling will help the congregation focus on disciple development. Those with reservations and hesitancy about this calling or purpose will hold back, retarding the congregation's progress in becoming a disciple-forming community. Typically, pastors don't do this consciously. On the other hand, what leaders believe and embrace tends to play out in the congregation over time.

How does embracing a disciple-developing perspective influence day-to-day ministry for pastors?

Most congregations are designed with an organizational model based on membership. Membership is not a biblical concept but is borrowed from the way organizations in North American culture tend to structure themselves. We are members of a credit union, service organizations, professional associations, and sailing clubs. With membership come certain rights, privileges, and responsibilities. There is nothing wrong with membership; it's simply not a biblical concept.

Pastors who buy into the membership perspective relate to church members in that way. Considerations include who is in and who is out, what membership means or doesn't mean, and especially how to get more members. If the pastor is interested in growing the church, then this means recruiting more members. These pastors consider membership numbers a primary indicator the church is spiritually growing and on track. They may or may not be interested in one's continuing growth after signing up for membership.

Disciple-developing pastors don't think this way. They are focused on helping disciples move forward in following Christ. They invest in individuals and groups in the congregation for the purpose of encouraging movement toward Christian maturity. They see the activities of the church as tools for strengthening, initiating, and inspiring disciple development. In some ways church membership becomes a minor factor for these pastors. They are interested in one's development throughout the Christian journey. They see developing disciples as an essential and central focus of their ministries. When disciples are developing, most likely they are far more invested in the church as an organization. Membership can come and go, but discipleship is an expression of who we are.

Does one need to be a Certified Disciple Development Coach to be a disciple-developing pastor? Of course not. Through the centuries many pastors have equipped the saints for ministry. Will your congregation more fully embrace the disciple-developing perspective if your pastor is trained in *DDC*? We believe *DDC* is a great tool to help pastors refocus their ministries as well as learn a model for doing what they are called to do: disciple development. When pastors engage in *DDC* training they are galvanized and focused on this essential ministry function, contributing to the congregation becoming a disciple-developing congregation.

Church Staff Commitment

When the pastor is committed to developing disciples, the door is opened for associate pastors and program staff to develop disciples. When the pastor is focused elsewhere, other staff can develop disciples, yet in a limited way.

The fastest way to know if your church staff is focused on developing disciples is to examine their job descriptions and the criteria for their annual evaluations. Too often the criteria are direct service oriented. Staff ministers are asked to provide Bible studies, run ministries, organize events, and meet the individual needs of congregational disciples. These are good activities, yet they may or may not develop disciples.

Most church staff members, along with their pastors, know the organizational needs of the congregation drive their evaluations. If the church is advancing in the three Bs—buildings, bodies, and budgets—a favorable evaluation results. If not, then concerns are raised. These criteria are organizationally driven, and they may support the church accomplishing its mission. At the same time, they may be inconsistent with a disciple-developing congregation's aspirations. When the three Bs are the de facto criteria, then savvy church staff members will hold the reins tightly, controlling for quality.

Equipping others to serve is a great concept, but when our annual evaluation rides on the quality of that service, we want control. These dynamics drive most church staff to function as direct service providers rather than equippers of the saints. Programming and administration are essential to service the organizationally driven church.

Disciple-developing congregations shift job descriptions to focus on the central task. These congregations expect their staff to invest in lay leadership, lay service, and lay involvement in missional ministries. These congregations evaluate effectiveness on how many lay persons served rather than on the quality of the staff person's direct service. When more people are discovering their callings and living out their faith day to day, then the disciple-developing staff person is serving effectively. The more the staff person is behind the scenes coaching others, the more successful disciple development becomes. Yes, this requires humility on the staff person's part. If she wants to be a rock star, then developing disciples won't happen. But if she receives permission from the church and person-ally believes the alternate approach best serves the church, then disciple development can happen.

We are describing a shift in the structure of a congregation, such as in job descriptions and evaluations for staff, yet an even greater shift must happen. Each staff person must be convinced that developing disciples is his calling, thus opening the way for a seismic shift in perspective. The role of church staff persons would change as follows:

• Become talent scouts and gift identifiers
• Call persons out, not for bad behavior but for their strengths and gifts.
• Become disciple developers in outlook
• Think about how others can live more fully into their callings
• Ask questions and explore options with persons in order to draw them forward in their spiritual journey
• Partner with God to help the kingdom to come more fully by seeing the potential for life and service in congregational disciples

A pastor and staff who are committed to developing disciples make vital contributions to the congregation's journey toward becoming a disciple-developing congregation.

Laity Commitment

The pastor who is trained in *DDC* will likely have a coaching relationship with the chair of the lay leadership team, whether formal or informal. As the chair experiences the energy and strength of *DDC*, she will want this for others. There are many dedicated and committed lay persons in churches all across the world who function as leaders (deacons, elders, vestry, council) in congregations. Frequently they are trained in how to manage the church, resulting in managerial leadership. Infrequently they are trained to develop the disciples in the congregation. With only minor exposure to the concept and experience of disciple development, lay leaders readily want more. Like ordained clergy and church staff, they see disciple development as a primary calling of God's church. Simultaneously, many lay leaders want tools to help them go deeper in their leadership and in their relationships with other disciples.

The following are ways to encourage lay leaders to shift their perspectives toward disciple development.

Provide a series of **DDC** *sessions for each team member upon beginning service.*

Remember, the power of *DDC* for transformation comes through experience rather than description. What a great way to facilitate a strong start to one's term on the lay leadership team. The lay leader sets the agenda and goals, not limiting the goals to serving in one's leadership role. Over time, engaging in three to four *DDC* sessions with the congregation's disciple development coach becomes an expectation of each lay leader.

Provide a **DDC** *class for the lay leadership team.*

After completing the class, these leaders will naturally begin using what they learn with the teams, committees, and groups with whom they relate. Part of the class is coaching a "buddy" in order to learn the model. As leaders coach each other toward living out their callings more fully, they are energized—not to mention the structure, programmatic, and financial shifts this would bring to their leadership. The focus of developing disciples moves to the front and center as a result of experiencing *DDC*. Church staff may find the first year that lay leaders will need to be asked to take the *DDC* class on a voluntary basis, knowing this was not part of the expectation when they agreed to serve. By the second year, it will probably be easy to include this class in the expectations as leaders have witnessed the benefits to their peers who have experienced *DDC*.

Ask the lay leaders to work on two growth goals: one unrelated to their service in the church and one related to their service as a lay leader.

This is being more directive with **DDC** than the model encourages. On the other hand, this approach combines some performance coaching with **DDC** in order to help the lay leadership team serve effectively. Many lay leaders will naturally choose a goal related to their service on the team.

Learning and growing leaders are invigorated leaders. As lay leaders make progress toward personal and service-oriented goals, their energy and enthusiasm increase. One can imagine the influence invigorated lay leaders will contribute to the congregation's mission and ministry. Some of these lay leaders will request certification, wanting to become **DDC** coaches themselves. In the meantime, they can practice developing disciples in their ministries.

Congregational Commitment

What would it be worth to you to see many disciples in your congregation engaged in substantive, transformational conversations around growth goals? This is what **DDC** is all about. Many disciples in congregations hunger for relationships that will support and challenge them to become the disciples Christ is calling them to be. For many, a few hours of Bible study and worship each week simply aren't enough to call out their best contributions to God's kingdom. Many of us hunger for more.

At this point the pastor, church staff, and lay leadership may have all engaged in **DDC** (or at least support it). It's likely that the grapevine is communicating effectively about the benefits of participation. If you have engaged **DDC** in the previously noted ways, you likely will have many people asking when they can have a chance to learn **DDC**.

Implementation and Reflection Questions

1. Who are the people in your life who care about you and want you to flourish so much that they will challenge you to rise up and be your best self?
2. The motto or tag line of **DDC** training is "coaching every ready disciple." Who in your congregation may be "ready"? Who is on the verge

of living into his faith journey at another level? Might this person be ready for a *DDC* coach?

3. Consider the pastor and church staff in your congregation. What priority do they give to developing disciples? How can you help them to consider investigating the *DDC* movement?

Using Coaching to Develop Disciples

"This is getting out of control!"

I (Mark) was consulting with a lay leadership team, pastor, and church staff about emerging ministries in their congregation. This enlivened church was experiencing something other churches long for: Lay persons were starting ministries without prompting from the church leaders. The church itself was encouraging attentiveness to God's Spirit and a permission-giving attitude. Disciples were encouraged to listen to the Spirit's whisper (or shout) and then to follow. As a result, new initiatives and ministries were emerging before their eyes. One lay leader who was used to the church's former organizational approach made the exclamation above. My heart sang when after a short pause another lay leader across the room said in a strong happy voice, "Yes, it is getting out of control—and thanks be to God." As the conversation continued, this team and its pastor decided this is what they were hoping for: Spirit-led missional activity.

This is also our hope for *DDC* in congregations. Once a certified *DDC* coach is in place teaching classes, then disciples in the congregation will naturally (apparently spontaneously) engage others in coaching. This is the nature of a congregational movement. Informal spontaneous activity is beyond anyone's control—"thanks be to God."

While this is happening, the congregation can continue its formal intentional *DDC* ministry. As previously described, teaching *DDC* classes is the place to begin. Certified coaches can teach any number of classes in their congregations—yearly, quarterly, monthly. As often as a critical mass is ready, another class can be offered and completed. This is the most effective, formal method for integrating *DDC* into congregations. Yet this is not the only intentional, formal method for implementing the wisdom and usefulness of *DDC*.

The following examples are uses for *DDC* in the congregational context. You will quickly recognize the versatility for use of *DDC* in congregational life. As you are reading, you may recognize that implementation requires a more detailed understanding than what is described here. Due to the scope and limitations of this book, we are not able to provide comprehensive descriptions (the *DDC* course includes details trainers will need to know). This chapter will give you direction and inspiration when considering how your congregation may use *DDC*.

Forming and Staffing a *DDC* Coaching Ministry

How is the disciple care system in your congregation structured? (We use the phrase "disciple care" to describe what is often called "pastoral care" or "member care"—moving away from the membership model.) Congregations designate persons and groups to respond to the individual care needs of the congregation. Stephen ministers are an example of an effective disciple care ministry.

But what about those people who need something more oriented toward growth, goal achievement, and action? They may not be hurting or needing a "care" type of visit. Instead, these disciples are ready to grow and move ahead in their spiritual journeys. Their need is for an able companion on their disciple journey rather than supportive care. This is when a cadre of trained disciple development coaches is very helpful. Often these ready disciples initiate conversations with pastors and church staff, who then can immediately connect the disciples before them with appropriate *DDC* coaches. The disciples learn about the congregation's *DDC* ministry and how it works. No fee is involved. This is simply a ministry of the church. Your congregation's *DDC* coordinator may be the contact person who connects disciples with coaches.

Choosing a Coordinator

Below we will describe various ways to use *DDC* to advance the mission and ministry of your congregation. Effective use of *DDC* will lead to numerous coaching relationships and activities. You will need someone to coordinate this ministry. We consciously use the word "coordinate" since this person will not be providing the bulk of the coaching. Disciples in the congregation coach each other. Once disciples are trained, a movement begins that is beyond anyone's control. Thus, much coaching will occur spontaneously as the need arises without any human coordination. At the same time, specific *DDC* ministries will develop. These will need coordination in order to maximize their benefit.

Establishing Ongoing Coaching Relationships

During the *DDC* class, participants are placed in pairs with a "buddy" coach. They meet bi-weekly to coach each other toward growth goals using the *DDC* model. Buddy coaching is built into the experience of the class. The benefits of coaching are more caught than taught. When disciples experience the power of *DDC*, they are engaged. Learning to coach involves instruction and conceptual thinking. Even more, *DDC* is learned through doing. These coaching pair relationships provide the context for safe learning opportunities as disciples practice *DDC*.

When the class is over, many of these coaching buddy pairs will naturally continue. Often near the end of a class, disciples will ask if they "have to stop coaching each other when the class is over." Of course not—and we hope not. Now they know each other well, have shared much with each other, and want to continue coaching. Many of these pairs established for the sake of "learning the *DDC* model" continue in established coaching relationships. Eventually, they may no longer meet on a schedule but continue to maintain an open coaching relationship. Whenever the need arises for coaching, they get together. Developing a culture of coaching every ready disciple encourages *DDC* coaches to be ready when the next ready disciple surfaces.

Integrating New Disciples into Congregational Life and Ministry

Early in this book we described the emerging hunger of people in congregations for hands-on involvement in missional ministry. Fewer disciples are satisfied with sending money to far-off mission fields as their only expression of love for God's world. More want to go themselves or serve in their local communities. Few post-modern disciples are willing to sit through unproductive committee meetings, but they are ready to engage in productive service that contributes to God's kingdom.

Because of this emerging dynamic, we frequently are asked how to engage newcomers to congregations. The former word for this activity was "assimilation," outdated because of its connection to outdated organizational language. Now we talk in terms of integration. How do we integrate newcomers into missional service, congregational community life, and the many other aspects of this congregation?

Proactive congregations conduct new member classes or inquirer classes. Traditional classes may happen on Sunday mornings before worship for the purpose of learning about the congregation. Some congregations even do a spiritual gifts inventory as a part of the process, helping disciples identify their gifts for service.

Can you imagine the depth, connection, and growth opportunity for newcomers when **DDC** becomes a component of their integration into this congregation? The **DDC** coach invests in this new disciple's calling, gifts, passion, and life journey. The focal question becomes, "Given your personal life journey and your current life context, what is God's calling for you now?" Of course the **DDC** coach is not looking for a particular answer. The goal is not to get this newcomer to fill an open position in the church structure. The goal is to help this disciple live out her calling more fully. Often, perhaps typically, one expression of this calling will be service through the congregation. At the same time, her calling involves all of her life.

When a congregation really becomes a disciple-developing congregation, newcomers may choose to participate in a **DDC** class as a part of their integration process.

Coaching Ministry Teams, Task Forces, and Committees to Accomplish Their Missions

Being part of a church is basically a communal experience. The Bible uses metaphors such as the body to describe how interconnected disciples are in churches. Thus, many activities congregations do are team based. Whether you are the pastor, a church staff person, or a lay person, those involved in a congregation will probably serve through and with many teams—whatever the name (committee, ministry team, men's group, women's circle, youth group, or children's ministry).

Since working with and through teams is integral to congregational life, you will find ready use for **DDC** in relation to teamwork. Teams function all along the continuum from ineffective to effective. **DDC** can help teams identify their purpose, gain traction, and complete their mission.

Below are common challenges of team functioning. Disciples trained in the **DDC** model can use **DDC** questions to guide teams toward effectiveness, whether they are the identified team leader or not. Following are some challenges teams face and **DDC** actions to help meet each challenge:

Start a meeting with the outcome in mind.
- Ask: "What do we want to accomplish through this meeting?"
- Ask: "What do we want to gain as a result of meeting for the next forty-five minutes?"
- Ask: "If we could fast forward to the end of this meeting and everyone around this table said the meeting was effective, what would we have done?"

Develop workable goals for the team.
- Explore: Introduce SMART goals. "Is this team's goal SMART?"

Lead problem-solving discussions.
- Explore: Use any of the "explore" tools. "When we pause and listen to the still small voice in the back of our minds, what do we hear about this dilemma?"

Measure progress.
- Explore: Focus on SMART goals again.
- Ask: "Remember what we identified at the beginning of our meeting as our goal for this meeting? How well are we progressing toward that goal?"
- Explore: "On a scale from 0-10, where were we in accomplishing our task as a team last meeting? Where are we now on the same scale?"

Forward the action.
- Design: "What's our next step?"
- Commit: "How ready are we to commit to this action?"
- Commit: "How much of a priority is accomplishing this action between now and the next time we gather?"
- Support: "What do we need from God and from each other to actually do this?"

Cast a vision.
- Explore: "If we really let go of this and the Holy Spirit moves through it, what might happen?"
- Explore: "If we imagine looking at this from God's perspective, what might we see?"
- Listen: "Deep down in our hearts, what are we hoping for around this project?"

Troubleshoot.
• Explore: Use any of the tools in the "explore" step
• Explore: "Suppose the barriers to progress on this project disappeared, what would we do then? What's that telling us?"

Stay on task.
• Ask: "Are we accomplishing what we said at this meeting's beginning?"
• Ask: "How likely is it that we will accomplish our goal for this meeting?"

Another way to visualize using **DDC** with teams is to consider each **DDC** step and potential questions for teams, groups, or committees. We give significant attention to this activity in the **DDC** certification course.

Providing *DDC* Groups

Some **DDC** coaches may organize and facilitate **DDC** coaching groups. As one might expect, coaching a group is much more complex than doing **DDC** with an individual or even as a part of a team's process. There are many dynamics and processes happening in a coaching group that require fairly developed **DDC** skills. Our advice is not to begin **DDC** with a group but to become proficient with individuals and working teams and then move to groups.

When the coach is ready, providing a **DDC** group is an energizing and encouraging experience and also an excellent way to advance the **DDC** movement in one's congregation. Research regarding particular mental health and addiction issues identifies group counseling as the most effective treatment available. Though **DDC** is far different in its purpose, the power of groups is amazing. I (Mark) have facilitated many kinds of groups throughout my ministry journey and am consistently reminded of their influence. Now we are very excited about the potential payoff in the lives of disciples when they gather in groups, using the **DDC** approach to growth.

Enhancing Preaching and Teaching

Preaching is typically one-way communication—from the preacher to the congregation. Given this, how can the *DDC* conversation be relevant to preaching? This is an astute question. There are several aspects of preaching where principles from coaching can further the action or integrate the message. Preachers can consider the following suggestions, perhaps even trying them on for fit.

Cultivate the coaching perspective.

    DDC is a tool with specific techniques. On the other hand, *DDC* is a perspective or mindset—an attitude about life. A major aspect of the *DDC* perspective is curiosity. Curiosity about life, God, people, and the Scriptures leads to transformational preaching filled with insights and meaning. Preachers who cultivate the *DDC* mindset and perspective will add depth and breadth to their sermons, exploring questions such as these:

- What is life about?
- What is God up to in this world?
- How are people put together?
- What makes people the way they are?
- How does God interact with people and our lives?
- What does following in the way of Jesus look like?
- What does it mean to live as a disciple?
- How do disciples relate to each other when in a group?
- What distinguishes a community of Jesus followers?

Use questions.

    Proclaimers of the gospel have used powerful questions for years to focus the attention of listeners around a central theme or point. *DDC* provides questions especially relevant to certain aspects of church life often addressed in preaching. One pastor who I (Mark) coached wanted to help those in his congregation discern God's calling for the next season of ministry. They entered a discernment time, considering their focus for life together and ministry in their community. This pastor tweaked the miracle question to stir the imaginations of the congregation: "Suppose this year that God gave us all the resources we ever needed to accomplish his calling for this church. What would we do?" Look through the

DDC questions in this book. You will find numerous questions relevant to preaching and teaching.

Ask for responses.

What's the purpose of preaching or proclaiming the gospel? The Gospel writers were purposeful with their words, as in these verses from John: "Now Jesus did many other signs in the presence of his disciples, which are not written in this book. But these are written so that you may come to believe that Jesus is the Messiah, the Son of God, and that through believing you may have life in his name" (vv. 30-31). By recording the acts of Jesus, the Gospel writer sought to persuade the reader that Jesus is the Messiah and Savior. Sermons in our time have a similar purpose: to persuade. Some congregations ask worshippers to respond to God's movement at the end of worship in an altar call or invitation. One way to "further the action" is to ask worshippers to respond to God's prompting in a tangible way the following week. "We want to invite you to respond to this message in a tangible way. This week consider writing out your response and emailing it to the church office or to the pastor. We believe this will help us integrate God's word for us today more fully."

*Begin and end worship with a **DDC** question.*

As the service begins, ask: "What are you here to gain today?" (Make room for silent reflection, after inviting worshippers to reflect on this question.) At the conclusion of the service, ask: "What are you taking away from this service today?" (Silent reflection) Worship is not primarily about us; worship is about God. So, the next week begin the service with: "What are you here to give to God today?" (Silent reflection) As the service concludes, ask: "What did you give to God through worship today?" (Silent reflection) These kinds of coaching activities around worship heighten the opportunity to become active participants in worship while also integrating the experience into our lives.

DDC as Leadership Development

The goal of *DDC* is growth, transformation, and maturing as disciples of Jesus Christ. The goal of *DDC* is not functioning effectively in our leadership positions nor developing leaders. We at Pinnacle do leadership coaching, which is focused on leadership growth and effectiveness. But this is not the purpose of *DDC*.

Simultaneously, leaders may be strengthened and developed as a result of gains made through their experience of **DDC**. Leadership development is more of a by-product than a purpose.

To clarify the distinctions, consider the contrasts between performance coaching and **DDC**. Performance coaching is useful for anyone in a supervisory position. **DDC** is useful in more of a peer relationship. Consider the contrasts in the chart below.

PERFORMANCE COACHING	DISCIPLE DEVELOPMENT COACHING
Supervisory role with some authority	Not an authority-based relationship
Has a direct stake in the outcome	Has less of a stake in the outcome
Has a goal of improved vocational performance	Has a goal of living into one's calling

Performance coaching has its place in Christian ministry. Pastors and church staff who supervise others can use performance coaching to support progress and effectiveness of supervisees in their respective ministries. Pastors may engage lay leaders with performance coaching when help is needed to function well in one's role. With each of these examples, the one doing the coaching has an agenda: She wants the performance of the supervisee or lay leader to go well. The one coaching has expectations for performance, along with a responsibility to intervene if the supervisee or lay leader goes way off track. The pastor or staff supervisor may use the **DDC** conversation and tools in coaching supervisees and lay leaders. At the same time, the pastor or supervisor must be aware and acknowledge when reaching out to performance coaching to address particular concerns. Focusing on the items in the contrasting chart above gives guidance when questions arise about what kind of coaching is needed.

Implementation and Reflection Questions

1. Consider your participation in teams, whether in church or elsewhere. How well do they function? What tools from *DDC* might you use to sharpen the focus of these teams or to advance their progress?

2. The authors suggest a congregation secure a *DDC* coordinator. Could you see yourself serving in this role? Would you be interested in connecting those with a coaching need with a disciple development coach who could meet that need?

3. How ready is your congregation for something like *DDC*? How might you go about introducing the coaching approach to disciple development?

Epilogue

"If you want to build a ship, don't summon people to buy wood, prepare tools, distribute jobs, and organize the work, rather teach people the yearning for the wide, boundless ocean."
—*Antoine de Saint-Exupery*[1]

Can you imagine what might happen if every ready disciple in every ready congregation received coaching?

- When a disciple expresses a spiritual hunger and desire to grow in faith, the church has a specific way to help her move ahead.
- When new people come into this faith community, the church has a specific way to help them discover where they will fit in and their places of service.
- When a disciple describes an unresolved concern that eats away at his well-being and distracts from living fully, the church has a specific way to help him address this concern and take action.
- When an overwhelming challenge arises for a disciple, the church has a specific way to offer her support and accountability through a Spirit-based process.

When **DDC** is available to every ready disciple, then the church is engaging Christian formation at an entirely new level.

Why are we so excited about **DDC** and its potential? Our experience in teaching the foundational course and practicum to clergy, church staff, and laity confirms the usefulness of **DDC** for addressing formational needs. Their resulting enthusiasm and excitement as they coach disciples in their context are inspiring. But why are these people resonating so well with **DDC**? Three streams seem to be flowing together to create a powerful flow around **DDC**.

The Commission and Calling of the Church

First, the church is called to make disciples. Other organizations in the world do fine activities, contributing to the world's progress. But the church is the one organization whose primary purpose is to make disciples of Jesus Christ. When the church's purpose becomes something else, it typically experiences decline in vigor, power, and participation.

Ephesians 4:12-13 describes the role of the church and its gifts in relation to Christian disciples this way: "to equip the saints for the work of ministry, for building up the body of Christ, until all of us come to the unity of the faith and of the knowledge of the Son of God, to maturity, to the measure of the full stature of Christ." This is a primary calling of God's church: to help Christian disciples mature toward the full stature of Christ.

While previous methods of Christian formation have been helpful, they are not sufficient for the formational needs of post-modern disciples. *DDC* helps us do what we are called to do as God's church. It is not a perfect approach or the only process for developing disciples. Yet *DDC* is a strong tool for advancing the Christian journey to which we are all called. Within *DDC* is the capacity for connecting with disciples at whatever stage they may be on the journey.

The Contextual Challenges to the Church's Mission

The church is facing unprecedented change and challenges. Former church models, structures, practices, and cultures do not work well today. Declining church participation in every denominational and non-denominational setting tells us so (although it's not all about numbers). The organized church is losing ground in its efforts to connect the good news of Christ with a spiritually hungry world.

Given the situation in which we live, it is time to engage in adaptive change in church life. *DDC* is not *the answer*. It is a relational process for discovering the answers, however. It is focused on growth, transformation, and discovery. These are the activities the church needs in order to meet the challenges of its current context.

Openness to Doing Christian Formation Differently

As we speak, I (Mark) am consulting with a church about initiating weekly small group gatherings in homes rather than investing in building the church's midweek gathering at the church building. Why are the leaders interested in and willing to push through the turmoil of change this initiative brings? They want to adapt their approach to the culture wherein they now find themselves. Their former approach worked well for forty years, but newer disciples to this congregation don't relate to the midweek church gathering as those who are used to this model of church. This church is open to new, culturally sensitive ways of expressing itself. *DDC* helps cultivate a church culture that embraces adaptive change.

There is another aspect of *DDC* for which we are discovering much openness. *DDC* is not designed to be a clergy or church staff ministry. While clergy and church staff are involved and supportive, and some even become certified disciple development coaches, the aim of *DDC* is to coach every ready disciple in the congregation. No pastor or church staff person could meet this goal. If we cling to the outdated belief that the pastor and church staff must provide all the transformational ministries in our congregation, then we will constrain the Holy Spirit's movement. When we equip multiple persons in the congregation to coach others, then we begin a movement not dependent on one person. It seems that entire congregations—clergy, church staff, and laity—are open to this approach more now than ever before. The lay persons we are training to become coaches are enthusiastic about serving in this role. Even now they are teaching *DDC* classes in their local congregations.

DDC is not *the* answer to the post-modern dilemmas of Christ-followers and Christian congregations. *DDC* is about dreaming dreams, seeing visions, and discovering new pathways in one's journey as a Christ-follower. We believe that disciples who turn their faces to the wind of the Holy Spirit are those who will have the eyes to see and the ears to hear as God's kingdom emerges. *DDC* is a mindset, a perspective, and a useful tool for positioning us in this holy breeze. May your journey of Christ-following, of orienting your life around the risen Lord, be blessed.

Note

[1]Quoted by Alan Hirsch, *The Forgotten Ways: Reactivating the Missional Church* (Brazos Press, 2009), 27.

Endorsements

"Jesus said to us (his followers), 'Go and make disciples.' As a Christian education pastor, I thought I was doing that by providing this course and that course. While most all of these courses are good, I have wondered if anything more than knowledge was gained.

"Across all Christian faith traditions we have equated "making disciples" with replicating orthodoxy or continuing tradition. It is true that knowledge can lead to change, but without a challenge either internal or external, one fails to actually live the knowledge. A disciple development coach helps the disciple apply biblical knowledge based on goals determined by the disciple.

"*Disciple Development Coaching* is not another course. It does not teach theology, doctrine, or church polity. It is a process in which disciples are coached in their faith walk. It is a one-on-one engagement of a disciple/follower of Christ assisting another in drawing out the ability within himself what he wants to do and be in order to be a disciple of Christ.

"I believe *Disciple Development Coaching* will be the start of a new paradigm of Christian education, a.k.a. 'making disciples,' in the current millennium and beyond."

—*Tommy Deal*
Pinnacle Leadership Associates
Disaster Response Coordinator, Cooperative Baptist Fellowship

"Mark Tidsworth and Ircel Harrison have given the church a tool for the times. Gradually and in diverse places, the church is reawakening to the fact that the mission of God focuses on God's dream, not human aspirations. That dream encompasses more than we can grasp, to be sure. Scripture helps us by calling God's plan the Reign (Kingdom) of God: the redemption of all creation and the realignment of life around God and God's ways. Followers of Christ cannot hurry God's redemptive design, but many are at work realigning their own lives around God and Christ. This is a chore in a culture that exalts individualism and autonomy; where personhood is defined by unencumbered choice; where freedom is to pursue one's self by choice and desire.

"The community of faith at Ephesus must have struggled similarly. The letter of Paul to the Ephesians lists gifts that God and Christ distributed among them. It then defines the purpose of these gifts as 'to equip the saints for the work of ministry, for building up the body of Christ, until all of us come to . . . maturity, to the measure of the full stature of Christ' (Eph. 4:12-13 NRSV). We are then told to put off the old self and to clothe ourselves 'with the new self, created according to the likeness of God in true righteousness and holiness' (vv. 22-24). To be sure, there is only one Christ. Still, we are, all of us, called to become more Christlike.

"Small groups and some congregations have embarked upon growing as faithful disciples and seek ways to be so formed. *Disciple Development Coaching* is a guide for those serious about accepting God's plan for their lives. Based on coaching strategies that help persons find strengths and growth practices within them, **DDC** charts the training of peer coaches who invite disciples into the development that God intends for each of God's children. Complete and based on solid practices, the book avoids the 'seven-step syndrome' of many programmatic growth offerings. Instead, it acknowledges the work of the Spirit in each one's life as well as the church and imparts skills for those who seek to open individuals and institutions to the work of that Spirit.

"*Disciple Development Coaching* is a timely gift for both the twenty-first-century church and disciples who take seriously God's call to grow into our true selves—the selves called to become more and more like Christ. The training outlined by Harrison and Tidsworth is a call and means for coaches, those coached, and the church to come closer to God's mission and plan for creation. This is a gift that has been worth the wait and deserves to be utilized for the sake of God's Reign."

—*Alan Arnold*
Executive Presbytery, Trinity Presbytery
Lexington, S.C

"Do you remember someone in your life who transformed the way you thought about your faith; someone who listened without judgment, encouraging you, lovingly asking just the right questions to cause you to think a little more?

"This is how I have experienced *Disciple Development Coaching* as it grows discipleship in the congregational setting. It is a very natural, yet intentional and focused way of accompanying others as disciples growing in their faith walk with Jesus. It's not a new program to add to the many other activities going in your congregation or personal daily list of "things to do." It is a process that can transform our understanding of what it means to disciple others on our journey as the body of Christ—naturally, yet with intentionality.

"It sounds so simple, yet what Ircel Harrison and Mark Tisdworth have put together is as clearly written, theologically based, and naturally focused as I have seen in my many years in ministry."

—*Martha Beahm*
Minister, Church of the Brethren
Licensed Marriage and Family Therapist

"Not that long ago a man came up with a simple equation that changed the world of physics. Einstein's $E=MC^2$ is a simple equation on the surface. Beneath the surface of its simplicity is its genius that changed the world of physics. This same Einstein is quoted by Mark Tidsworth and Ircel Harrison in the context of their concept, Disciple Development Coaching: 'Insanity is doing the same thing over and over again and expecting different results.'

"Disciple Development Coaching is simplicity on the surface that beneath is genius, offering the church a tool to move past its current insanity of continuing to do the same things over and over again and wondering why the truth of Jesus Christ continues to flounder in the world of the twenty-first century. If the missional church describes a community of disciples for the twenty-first century, then Disciple Development Coaching reveals the tool or mindset within the missional church.

"Tidsworth and Harrison introduce the reader to the basis, the basics, and the applications of Disciple Development Coaching in a clear and concise manner. Their book is a gift from the Spirit and a beginning for the church to become what Christ intended when he said to his followers, 'By this all will know that you are my disciples, if you have love for one another' (John 13:35)."

—*R. T. Byrne*
Pastor, St. Paul Lutheran Church
Aiken, S.C.

"Having read a number of books on coaching and discipleship, what I appreciate most about this book is the authors' clarity of why and how discipleship coaching fits the post-modern and post-Christendom context of our rapidly changing culture. In an easy-to-read format the authors offer clear tools, insightful questions, and helpful illustrations of how the coaching process can deepen the discipleship growth of congregational leaders and enhance the mission of the church. They do not offer a program or quick fix for declining congregations, but rather a relational approach that helps persons discover and live into a deeper sense of faithfulness to God's calling in their lives."

—*Herman R. Yoos*
Bishop, South Carolina Synod
Evangelical Lutheran Church in America

"*Disciple Development Coaching* is one of those rare books that educates and inspires. The wisdom of *DDC* is ancient, but the process is fresh and innovative. This is not a book on pastoral care, but it offers an approach that is caring and pastorally 'companioning.' This is not a book on spiritual direction, but the methodology it proposes is spiritually nurturing.

"If you want to stop attending meetings and start engaging in service, this book is for you. If you are ready to move your congregation from membership development to disciples' development, this book is for you. If you long to transform your ministry from purpose-drivenness to Spirit-led responsiveness, this book is for you. If you yearn for the Good News to stop being 'taught' and start being 'caught' and to move God's disciples from assimilation to integration; if developing disciples or being a disciple responsive to God's call is appealing to you, this book is for you."

—*Katheryn Graham*
Associate Minister, Kansas City Region
Disciples of Christ

"While the latest and greatest programs and the newest church fads typically suggest changes to the institutional ministry, *Disciple Development Coaching* addresses the reality of this statement as it focuses on the transformation of individual members. With its easy to use, step-by-step format, this book provides the knowledge and tools necessary for coaches to intentionally and skillfully guide others to unleash the power of their spiritual gifts upon the world. Through **DDC**, the people in your congregation can become the disciples they are created and called to be, thereby allowing your church to be everything God intends it to be."

—*Stephen Mims*
Pastor, Summer Memorial Lutheran Church
Newberry, S.C.

"If you are choosing one new adventure this year, *Disciple Development Coaching* is a transformative, exciting jaunt. Honest and practical, it is imminently helpful and decidedly user-friendly. Mark and Ircel have presented material and tools in such a focused way that you are not just captivated by the possibilities, but poised for action. A remarkable resource!"

—*Mikki Corley Gay*
New Church Developer, Breath of Life Lutheran Church
Blythwood, S.C.

"Here is usable and helpful wisdom on the emerging practice of disciple development coaching from two gifted practitioners of faith and leadership. With frontline experience on the pathways that lead people to deeper faith and transformational living, Mark and Ircel share their discoveries with us. I commend this book not only for your reading but also for your use."

—*Susan Leonard-Ray*
Anderson District Superintendent
United Methodist Church, South Carolina